WINNICOTT'S BABIES AND
WINNICOTT'S PATIENTS

WINNICOTT'S BABIES AND WINNICOTT'S PATIENTS
Psychoanalysis as Transitional Space

Margaret Boyle Spelman

KARNAC

First published in 2013 by
Karnac Books Ltd
118 Finchley Road
London NW3 5HT

British Library Cataloguing in Publication Data

A C.I.P. for this book is available from the British Library

ISBN-13: 978-1-78220-044-4

Typeset by V Publishing Solutions Pvt Ltd., Chennai, India

Printed in Great Britain

www.karnacbooks.com

For Ciana, Cara, Conor, and Claire

CONTENTS

ACKNOWLEDGEMENTS

I would like to acknowledge my debt of gratitude to the mother, the baby, and the family who feature most prominently here. I would also like to acknowledge my appreciation and indebtedness to the babies and families who have been my clients and patients in both my work as a psychologist and as a psychoanalytic psychotherapist.

I would like to recognise the help and support of the following:

Claire, Conor, Cara, Ciana, and Brian; Ian and Yvonne and Beda; friends Nathalie and Lelia; and colleagues Ross Skelton, Julie Carmody, (the late) Pat Holley, Mary Pyle, and Michael Fitzgerald.

ABOUT THE AUTHOR

Margaret Boyle Spelman is a registered clinical psychologist, a psychoanalytic psychotherapist, and an organisational psychologist. She has worked for three decades as a clinical psychologist in the Irish Health Services with particular interest in the areas of early intervention, parenting, and learning disability. She has been in private practice as a psychologist and psychotherapist since 1998.

Margaret is an Executive Member of the Irish Forum for Psychoanalytic Psychotherapy and a Board Director for the Irish Council for Psychotherapy and Vice-Chairperson for the Psychoanalytic Section of the Irish Council for Psychotherapy. She has Masters degrees in psychology from University College Dublin, Dublin City University, and in psychotherapy from Trinity College, Dublin and the Irish Institute of Psychoanalytic Psychotherapy. She completed her PhD at the Centre for Psychoanalysis, University of Essex, and is the author of *The Evolution of Winnicottís Thinking: Examining the Growth of Psychoanalytic Thought Over Three Generations.*

PREFACE

This book marks many beginnings. It retraces the beginning of my personal journey as a psychoanalytic psychotherapist and my simultaneous discovery of the thinking of D. W. Winnicott (1896–1971), paediatrician, psychiatrist, psychoanalyst, communicator, broadcaster, and writer.

This discovery, which is a continuing process, was of very great help to me then—and still is. My hope for this book is that it will facilitate others with their own versions of these kinds of beginnings. The other types of beginnings that might be the case here include a retracing of one's own beginnings in life, or of one's life as a parent, whether one is actually at the beginning of that career or at a progressed stage.

I found Winnicott's thinking to be of tremendous help to me when first I was a beginner psychotherapist. (I hope that I still am a beginning psychotherapist in my outlook!) My discovery of Winnicott's writing helped me distinguish my emerging working life at the time from my previous professional life as a clinical psychologist, often working with children of the nought to five age group and their parents.

It has been noted that with Winnicott's thinking, everyone has, and needs to have, his or her own personal response. It has often been said that everyone has their own "Winnicott". I hope that in sharing some of my early personal response to Winnicott that I will facilitate the reader in developing his or her own.

Also, because the prospect of doing a first baby observation was a daunting one, I include notes on a fictionalised composite baby observation in the hope that it is helpful in bringing Winnicott's thinking alive. My experience of baby observation has been a truly joyful one— and particularly in the case most featured here—but I know that I have been very fortunate and perhaps unusual in this. It is important to note that it is not always that way. Not only positive feelings of pleasure and joy are induced in the observer by what is observed.

It was a little strange for me going into what was ostensibly a familiar situation. I say "familiar" because in my life as a psychologist I had for years gone to see mothers and their very young child, or baby, at home—often making several visits of this kind in a week. I would arrive with my Bayley Infant Scales or equivalents, casually referred to as my "box of tricks", and occasionally accompanied by a psychologist in training. But those visits, with the emphasis on providing structured immediate support to the parents—and focusing on the baby's intellectual and adaptive development—seem as though they were in a parallel universe of a kind because here in the baby observation situation, although the scene was outwardly identical, there was a new emphasis and a new role. I was simply there to observe and the emphasis was on the emotional rather than developmental life of the infant. The vista was at once familiar and yet so profoundly new and scary, but nevertheless exhilarating.

In this book, I compare the "good enough" situation of the baby to early situations where there is a degree of what Winnicott refers to as "environmental deficit". These situations are looked at here in retrospect in the situation where they have ultimately resulted in an adult attending for psychotherapy. When discussing the therapy situation, I refer to "the therapist" of the theoretical discussion and "the therapist" of the clinical example. This means that I am sometimes referring to myself in the third person, as "the therapist". I do this so that the theoretical discussion and the clinical examples run together smoothly and I hope that it is not too distracting.

The example of the "good enough" situation of the baby is comprised here of a fictionalised/composite baby observation involving the fictionalisation and amendment of one particular baby observation, with added features which have arisen in others and from baby visits made for other reasons at other times. The baby observation provides an opportunity to look at the original developmental situation and to bring it fully alive. The adult examples allow us to view the deficit situation in the clinical/therapeutic situation. The first involves the "nursing couple" and the second involves the "analytic couple" or "therapeutic couple".

As I write, I feel privileged and grateful to my patients for the intimate view of their lives which they have shared in the course of their therapy. I am also very grateful to the family of the baby observation mostly involved here and to all the families who, in the course of my work, helped my learning. I wish to gratefully salute those families everywhere who volunteer to share this precious time in their family's and in their baby's life, and to acknowledge the very great value of what they contribute to the continued investigation of human nature and also to the business of making competent psychotherapists and psychoanalysts.

INTRODUCTION

Donald Woods Winnicott died in 1971 at the age of seventy-five, but his legacy is growing in importance. What accounts for this? What is it that makes Winnicott's thinking helpful and what is so special about his approach? What distinguishes it from what has gone before? This book attempts to go some way towards answering these questions. It also gives something of the experience of discovering Winnicott's thinking through a baby observation and through glimpses of the infant who remains and manifests in the adult patient.

One of the distinguishing features of Winnicott's thinking is that for him it is the relationship between the first dyad, commonly known as the mother and the baby together, which is of central importance to the formation of the individual person (or subject), to the particular nature of human experience, and to the nature of the relation to loved ones (or objects).

In psychoanalysis as it was developed by Freud, it is very clear that it is the Oedipus complex that is of great importance. We are told that for Freud the first phase of the baby's development is autoerotic, with the baby taking himself as the object of his own affections in what is called "primary narcissism". Eventually, by virtue of the pleasure experienced in feeding, the baby leaves autoeroticism and narcissism and takes the mother as his first love object and we have the beginnings of what is called object relations. Freud saw this first relation as the basis for all other love relationships—he considered this process to be a universal phenomenon.

Yet this first situation with the mother and the baby cannot continue indefinitely. In Freud's formulation a triangular situation ensues where the father intervenes to separate the baby from the mother. It is generally considered that this process ultimately helps the baby to take up an acceptable position in life which eventually leads to his being a distinct and law-abiding member of society.

In Freudian thinking, this model is internalised within the individual baby as the ego ideal and the superego, and the sexual instincts are then channeled such that they do not incur censure. This last statement summarises the process of sublimation, which is Freud's explanation for the non-climactic behaviours of daily experience. The explanation provided by the idea of sublimation was not adequate for Winnicott.

For Freud, psychoanalysis deals with neurosis, and all psychoneurotic illness has its origin in this triangular oedipal situation. The importance of the dyadic relation of the baby with the mother neither received the same emphasis in Freud's thinking nor did he attend sufficiently, in Winnicott's view, to an exploration of the nature of this first relationship and the traces that it leaves in the psyche.

Many questions remained for Winnicott: how does the baby get from this unintegrated autoerotic state at the beginning, to the one of Freud's emphasis, in which he is resigned to the facts that he cannot rival his father's affections for his mother and that he must wait for a similar relationship of his own in adulthood? What are the developmental stages that intervene? How does the baby get from a state in which he cannot tell the difference between his mother and himself, to this psychogenic stage in which he sees that he is one separate entity in a situation involving two others and in which he recognises that one of these, like himself, has a penis and one does not? It is difficult to see how the baby's subjectivity comes about or how this developmental stage manifests in analysis. For Winnicott, it sometimes seemed that Freud saw the significance of this stage as simply setting the scene for the important Oedipal stage.

Winnicott felt that there was a gap in Freud's theory at this developmental point. He felt that Freud was unclear and inconsistent in his explanations of what happens between autoeroticism and the first object choice. He believed, in contrast, that what happened between the mother and the baby was of very great importance for the development of the self and that it accounted for much individual difference. It is a central contention in this book that Winnicott's explanation of this stage, and its transitional nature, helps a great deal in clarifying and developing Freud's theories and filling in developmental gaps.

A central assertion is that, as Winnicott suggests, there is much in this first relationship which is important in an analysis or psychotherapy. I also propose that, by making explicit the parallels between the development of self at this dyadic point, as outlined by Winnicott, and the development of self in the relationship between the therapist and patient, there is much for a therapist to learn. For those of us involved in therapy, these parallels can expand our theoretical understanding, and our practice can be made much more flexible.

In the chapters that follow, I take Winnicott's thinking on human nature, the maturational process, and facilitating environment, as the context for this argument. I account here also for his concepts of transitional phenomena because they remain among the most enduring and important of Winnicott's innovative ideas. It is for this reason that I give specific attention to the parallels in the first transitional space between the mother and the infant on the one hand, and the space between the therapist and patient on the other.

In an effort to explore this parallel in detail, I use the comparison of fictionalised composite clinical vignettes taken from my adult caseload with examples taken from a fictionalised composite infant observation.

"Good enough" and "not good enough" examples and a baby observation

In his writing, Winnicott describes the "ordinary devoted", the "good enough" mother, and the "good enough" environment. He tells us that women need to be healthy to fall into that state of sensitive imaginative "reverie" and "holding" about the baby which he refers to as "primary maternal preoccupation". He tells us that some women can experience difficulty getting into this state and some have trouble with getting out of it. My feeling of good fortune in my experience of baby observation and in the case presented here stems, in part, from the fact that this infant's mother did both successfully, in my estimation. For her, the fact that this was likely to be her last baby, coupled with the fact that she enjoyed this stage of her life so much, made the task of saying goodbye to her child's babyhood at least as difficult as the welcoming of it. Overall, I consider the infant observation presented here as an example of a "good enough" experience. I believe that for the healthy development of her baby, this mother provided a facilitating environment which contrasts in an obvious way to the deficiencies in the environments of the examples from my adult cases, which are included.

Whilst the infant observation represents the "good enough" "ordinary devoted mother" and the developmental situation, the clinical examples represent the analytic space and those difficulties that result from deficient and non-facilitating environments. Although the baby observed in this infant observation is a girl, I have decided to observe Winnicott's convention of referring to the baby as "he" in the course of my theoretical discussion.

The book plan

In Chapter One, I look briefly at the roots of Winnicott's thinking in the work of Freud and Klein, his two main recognised psychoanalytic influences, and at the general climate which influenced him in the area of child development. It is worth remembering here that the proper and conventional referencing of the writing of those who influenced Winnicott was something of a weak spot for him and something that he knew, towards the end of his life, was important but which continued to be an area of special difficulty for him.

After this first chapter, further chapters are developed along the lines of the three stages of dependence posited by Winnicott: "absolute dependence", "relative dependence", and "towards independence".

In Chapter Two, I give an in-depth examination of Winnicott's idea of absolute dependence and look at those concepts he considered to be most pertinent to the laying down of the boundary of "self" in its original setting of the nursing couple. Here too, I look at the foundation which is a prerequisite for the growth of transitional space and then, also, we examine the difficulties to do with this stage as they manifest in the treatment room. In this way the parallel between the analytic and developmental spaces is explored with particular reference to the concepts of holding, being, primary maternal preoccupation, and setting.

In Chapter Three, I explore the transitional nature of the space that emerges between the mother and the baby. We see here that the central focus, in relative dependence, is on the way in which the first experience of relative dependence is a prototype for all "between" spaces including the one arising between the therapist and patient. The nature of relative dependence is explored in some detail using the clinical vignettes referred to earlier. Winnicott's important concepts introduced here include "the period of hesitation", "sensitive failing", and "doing".

In Chapter Four, I take the opportunity to treat the stage involved in what Winnicott refers to as one's going "towards independence". What is concerned here is the lifelong nature of the negotiation of fantasy and reality which is a necessary prerequisite to creative and enjoyable living. I look at the particular nature of Winnicott's understanding. He considers that analysis needs to be flexible in its starting point and also in its emphasis in order to account for the experience of the two whole persons that are the therapist and the patient. This examination of the parallel between the two processes, of development on the one hand and analysis on the other, is completed in the hope of showing that these are, in many ways, though certainly not in all, analogous in nature.

Chapter Five takes a look in detail at a baby observation, and at the experience of engaging in a baby observation. Chapter Six follows with a summarising and reflective report on the baby observation. The reader should now be able to look back at the chapters that treat Winnicott's thinking and compare the baby of the observation with the one who has appeared in the course of an adult therapy.

CHAPTER ONE

The root of Winnicott's thinking

I have already referred to the difficulty that Winnicott had in estimating and recording his influences. He always privileged the growth of his own thinking and it is not surprising then that Winnicott himself was also somewhat unclear as to the extent to which his own thinking originated in that of Freud and Klein. For this reason, and by way of introduction to Winnicott's thinking and its application, this chapter outlines how both of these theorists viewed the influence on the human psyche of early experience and how they considered what transpired between the first couple, that is, the mother and the baby. I explore in detail the model of early experience, the role of the mother, and the early formation of the ego. I then visit briefly the other influences in the area of child development which were prevalent at the time.

Freud's thoughts on early experience

We now take a closer look at what Freud thought of the time close to the beginning of life and the infant's relation to the mother. Nowadays it is widely known that Freud considered early experience in terms of stages of psychosexual development—that is, oral, anal-sadistic, and phallic, leading to genital. His thinking on early development and on the pre-genital organisation of the libido evolved when he traced the symptoms of neurotic adult patients back to their origins in infantile sexuality. In Freud's chronological theory of psychosexual development, he posited different possible fixation points, which explain the varied nature of the neuroses. Freud's explanations might be paraphrased along these lines: "this symptom relates to that difficulty experienced at that stage, etc".

In outlining the psychosexual stages of the development of the personality, Freud gives "autoeroticism" as the first and the lowest sexual stratum. It has no sexual aim and demands only local feelings and satisfactions. Freud explains that autoeroticism continues to exist as a separate current even when succeeded by allo-eroticism (eroticism directed towards another), when its main path is identified with the loved person. Freud (1914) indicates the difference between autoeroticism and narcissism when he says that the ego does not exist from the very first as a unity and "a new psychical action" has to take place to bring about narcissism. Laplanche and Pontalis (1973) draw the distinction between the independent and anarchical satisfaction of instincts which is characteristic of autoeroticism and the structured narcissistic taking of the ego in its entirety as a love object. They say that the difference is explained by the coincidence in time of the dominance of infantile narcissism with the first formation of the ego. They also suggest that this is a point of varying opinion and ambivalence in psychoanalytic thinking. Freud posited a "see-saw" relation between narcissistic libido and object-libido. He proposes that "the more one is employed the more the other becomes depleted" (1914, p. 76). He also suggests that an original libidinal cathexis to the ego persists and is related to object-cathexis.

Furthermore narcissism has been linked by Freud to homosexuality, psychotic depression, and schizophrenia (1905, 1917, 1911a). The original autoerotic and narcissistic phases are pre-object organisations of the libido. Laplanche and Pontalis suggest that Freud's (1921, 1923) further exploration of the nature of narcissism at the beginning of life leads to some theoretical dead ends. These include one which refers to the very transition which is a central subject of this book, that is, the transition from the unaware autoeroticism at the beginning of life all the way through to the Oedipal situation. The dead ends cause Laplanche and Pontalis to ask "how are we supposed to picture the transition from

a monad shut in upon itself to a progressive discovery of the object?"
(1973, p. 257). Speaking of pregenital organisation in general, Freud
says:

> What we see is a great number of component instincts arising from
> different areas and regions of the body, which strive for satisfaction
> fairly independently [...] These impulses which strive for pleasure
> are not all taken up into the final organisation of the sexual func-
> tion [...] You have heard how in the course of this long-drawn-out
> development several phases of preliminary organisation can be rec-
> ognised and also how this history of the sexual function explains its
> aberrations and atrophies. (1933a, p. 98)

In Freud's thinking, the mouth is the first erotogenic zone of the oral
phase. For the first and second year of life, the baby gets pleasure as
well as food from sucking at the breast. The anal-sadistic phase in the
second, third, and fourth years coincides with toilet-training and is to
do with the anal impulses, as well as the control of eliminatory functions. Freud agreed with Abraham (1927) that ambivalence can be seen
in both of these stages.

In the third or phallic phase the zone is the same in both sexes—the
penis and its female equivalent (Freud considered the clitoris to be a
"little penis"). The male organ attains importance at this stage, with
the vagina only gaining importance in the definitive sexual instinct
after puberty in the genital phase. Both boys and girls wish to give the
mother a baby or have a baby for her and the father is, at that stage,
a superfluous rival. The libidinal organisation is first established in each
case by the pleasure attaching to the execution of an instinctual urge.

For a boy, the discovery that the mother does not have a penis brings
about the dissolution of the Oedipus complex between five and six
years of age (Freud, 1924). He then enters latency by virtue of a number
of factors. These are: castration anxiety; the prohibition on incestu-
ous wishes and narcissistic activity; the establishment of the superego
through identification with parental figures; and finally, the ego ideal,
the promise of a "new edition" of the love object, an equivalent gratification in adulthood through identification with the father.

Freud explains that a girl's development takes a more complex route
with a change in both love object (from mother to father) and erotogenic zone (from clitoris to vagina) in adult sexuality. Freud was less

satisfied with his attempts to explain the evolution of women's sexual development. He sees the Oedipus complex as a haven in which the girl recovers from castration anxiety and therefore its dissolution is less definite, less complete, and often marked by difficulty in exchanging father for another love object. One can see from all of this that, for the most part, Freud looked to childhood rather than to babyhood, to the Oedipus complex rather than preoedipal organisation, for explanations of neuroses, individual difference, and personality structure.

For Freud, the ego develops out of the unconscious unstructured "id" which is the basis of the human psyche at birth. It develops along the lines of the instinctual structure of the libido. From the beginning, libidinal energy is invested either in the ego or in the object. Attachment is either of an "anaclitic" (based on its difference from the subject) or "narcissistic" (based on identification with the subject) nature, which Freud says "seeks for the subject's own ego and finds it in other people" (1905, p. 222).

Freud found that the ego's "self-preservative" instinct was not only aimed at warding off biological insults such as hunger or thirst, but that it also worked to preserve its sense of respectability and integrity. This is the basis of repression. The ego banishes contents which cannot be acknowledged. It orients the psyche to reality and to the need to adapt. Freud (1920) realised that the reality and pleasure principles are not antagonistic to each other to the extent that they are both aimed at the pleasure involved in the discharge of tension. However, he tried to explain phenomena which defy the pleasure principle, such as self-injurious behaviour, masochism, and the tendency which he witnessed in shell-shocked soldiers from the First World War to repeat their trauma over again each night in their dreams. This is when Freud proposed the death instinct. The aim of mental life is to reduce tension from internal or external sources. In summary, Freud's death instinct proposes that, given the principles of constancy, stability, and the tendency to return to an earlier state of inorganic inertia, the aim of all life is death.

On one of the few occasions when he writes specifically about the relationship between the baby and the mother, Freud speaks of the operation of the pleasure principle at birth. He suggests that in an attempt to avoid unpleasure the baby hallucinates satisfaction but the subsequent nonsatisfaction and disappointment lead to the introduction of reality, pleasant or not, and the reality principle. In a footnote, Freud explains the basis of the baby's dependence on the mother. He says:

It will rightly be objected that an organisation that was slave to the pleasure principle and neglected the reality of the external world could not maintain itself alive for the shortest time, so that it could not have come into existence at all. The employment of a fiction like this is however justified when one considers that the infant—*provided that one includes with it the care it receives from its mother*—does almost realise a psychical system of this kind. (1911b, p. 220, my emphasis)

Goldman (1993) traces the connections between Freud's and Winnicott's thinking, saying that what Freud put in this footnote is what Winnicott spent his working life explaining. The footnote does seem to emphasise the baby's absolute dependence on the mother at the beginning of life both for physical and psychical survival. As such, it pre-empts what we will see is Winnicott's idea of the baby's absolute dependence at the beginning of life.

There is yet another interactive construction of the mother/baby relationship put forward by Freud when he says "A mother would probably be horrified if she were made aware that all her marks of affection were rousing her child's sexual [drive] and preparing for its later intensity" (1905, p. 223). He further suggests that the mother would not feel badly if she knew how important and necessary sexual love is to general success in life—after all she is simply "fulfilling her task in teaching the child to love". Another point of interest is the active rather than passive involvement of the mother which is important in Freud's understanding of her role. The important role of early experience in the healthy development of the infant is also emphasised in a general way in Freud's (1905) basic premise that the human love object and sexual development are not predetermined in human beings as they are in other species but are open to what he refers to as "variation" and "aberration". In a certain way, Freud views childcare as the first seduction in which anxiety is stirred up by either the mother's over- or under-stimulation of the child's affection. And, of course, we remind ourselves here of the part of his thinking that was originally so controversial—the nature of this relationship is the same, for Freud, as sexual love.

The essential importance of this first relationship for Freud is encapsulated in the "Three Essays on Sexuality" when he says that "There are thus good reasons why a child sucking at his mother's breast has become the prototype of every love relation. The finding of an object is in fact a refinding of it" (1905, p. 222).

Freud also sees parental love as the revival and reproduction of the parent's own narcissism. The baby is to have everything that they did not have. The mother loves the baby as she loves herself, leading to Freud's reference to "His Majesty the baby" (1914, p. 85).

In "Femininity", Freud says that the girl's powerful love of her mother ends in hate and a turning to the father as love object. He also claims however, that we cannot really understand a woman unless we take full account of her preoedipal attachment to her mother. He asserts that we did not know that it "could be so rich in content, so long-lasting" and "could leave behind so many opportunities for fixations and dispositions" (1933b, p. 119). The existence of many kinds of relationship corresponds to the phases of infantile sexuality. It is as though in the baby's experience, the mother gave "too little milk" and therefore love, allowing the unwanted intruder of the next sibling to usurp all signs of maternal care, and she also prohibited pleasurable activity with the genitals. The deciding accusation in the girl's changing to the father as love object, however, is the mother's culpability for the girl's arriving into the world without a penis. As Freud sees it, the Oedipus complex overshadows the preoedipal organisation for a time but both organisations are important in fact and both can yield permanent fixations. It is just a further small step to assume that Freud attributed such importance to the preoedipal organisation of the boy child as well as to the girl.

Klein's thoughts on early experience

Melanie Reizes Klein (1882–1960) became interested in child analysis when encouraged by her first analyst, Ferenczi. She worked with young children as well as adults developing her play technique and stressing the importance of the relationship to the breast. Mrs. Klein is responsible for the development of one of the three schools of thought in the British Psychoanalytical Society (Grosskurth, 1986). Klein's central focus was the understanding of anxiety and she sees anxiety as being present from birth. Klein's thinking, though not developed or published in that order, is best understood when considered in terms of the chronological development of the infant from birth. In stark contrast to Freud's, Klein's infant is born with the internal conflict of the life and death drive and with an idea of and a relationship to a person or part-person, such as the penis or breast (Mitchell, 1991). Klein (1952) says that there are rapid fluctuations in the infant's emotional life. The infant swings between love and hate, external and internal situations, perceptions of reality and the phantasies relating to it. Klein's neonate goes between persecutory anxiety and idealisation of both internal and external objects.

The infant's psychical world operates according to the biological processes of ingestion and excretion. Klein (1946) conceptualises four early mechanisms (Hinshelwood, 1991). Let us look briefly at each. In splitting, the ego can stop the bad part of the object from contaminating the good part by dividing it off (into the "good breast" and the "bad breast"), or it can split off and disown part of itself. In projection, the ego fills the object with some of its own split-off feelings and experiences. In introjection the ego takes into itself what it perceives or experiences of the object. In projective identification, a concept which has since been expanded by others, the ego projects its feelings into the object and then identifies with it, becoming like the object which, in phantasy, it has already filled with itself. The ego uses these four different defences to cope with the interaction between inner and outer worlds. From birth, the ego and the object are divided through splitting. Both the ego and the object are split to keep the benevolent satisfying breast from the malevolent frustrating one. This is why splitting occurs at birth and also why it continues throughout life as part of the health and pathology of the psyche. This is what Klein refers to as the paranoid-schizoid position.

The paranoid-schizoid position is the position from birth. The bad breast, representing bad experience, having been projected out, is felt to be an outside persecutor and splits into many subsequent pieces, becoming the many persecutors of paranoia. In order to satisfy the life instinct, the ego also projects part of the libido outwards, creating a "good object" outside so that now there is an "ideal object" and a bad persecutory object. The baby fears retaliation—the envied and hated breast becomes the envying and hating breast. This earliest paranoid-schizoid position of the neonate was the last to be written about by Klein. According to Klein (1957), there is no synthesis of love and hate, no easy interaction of the different parts of the mind, no fluid boundary between conscious and unconscious. There is a rigid barrier and the position is characterised by a fragmented, schizoid ego, and good and bad "part" objects.

With greater maturity the actual "whole" nature of the object is increasingly perceived, the good and bad objects begin to be synthesised.

This depressive position begins, according to Klein (1935, 1940), at between four and six months. For Klein, repression—which allows part of the mind to go in an integrated state into the unconscious— begins at this later stage. Now the good and bad aspects of the ego and objects come into contact with each other. The baby feels that, in frustration, he has damaged the mother he loves and he fears losing his good internal and external objects. These two positions continue throughout life with a reversion to a paranoid-schizoid position continuing as a response in certain stressful situations.

With regard to the effect of early experience on the baby, Klein considered the developmental path as being preset, for the most part, by constitutional factors. However, the ratio of frustrating to gratifying experiences of the object in the early days will determine the tendency towards splitting and the early mechanisms in later life. This ratio, and the opportunity to make reparation and restore the now damaged but "good" whole mother in the depressive position, will determine the propensity for omnipotent phantasy and a disavowal of the importance of the object in what Klein saw as the manic defence of the depressive position. The opportunity in early experience to trust and internalise a good object is important although Klein saw the child's development as weighted by innate aspects such as the death drive. As we will see, Klein gave less attention to the role of experience and to individual difference than did Winnicott.

Until 1934, Klein described her findings in terms of the Freudian structure of the id, ego, and superego and in terms of libidinal stages. When she posited the positions she departed from his theory. She found much earlier evidence of oedipal phantasies with a combined parental figure and pregenital aspects, and also of a superego with savage oral, urethral, and anal qualities. Klein (1932) reported on child cases where the severe parental imagos, reflecting the child's own sexual phantasies, would paralyse the child's play and daily activities.

Winnicott's perspective on his origins

The life of Donald Woods Winnicott (1896–1971) is well documented (Kahr, 1996; Phillips, 1988; Rodman, 2003). He first became interested in psychoanalysis when he read the "Interpretation of Dreams". He was twenty-three and already a medical doctor. His first analyst, James Strachey, and his second, Joan Riviere, were both analysed by Freud and were considered to be Kleinians for the most part. Winnicott had supervision with Klein when he began treating children and, like her (and by contrast to Anna Freud as we shall see shortly), believed that the analysis of children was the same as that of adults.

In 1923, Winnicott undertook two appointments, working as assistant physician at the Queen's Hospital, Hackney, in London's East End and at Paddington Green Children's Hospital (his "Psychiatric Snack Bar"), where he worked for over forty years until 1963. This became the core of his clinical practice. Winnicott became a paediatrician and a psychoanalyst and was also the first male child psychoanalyst in Britain. He was also a prolific writer, public speaker, and broadcaster. He was a member of the "Middle" group, now called the School of Independents, of the British Psychoanalytical Society of which he was twice president (Kahr, 1996). Unlike Freud, who extrapolated his theory of human development from his experience of adults, Winnicott was a children's doctor who in the course of his career saw 60,000 mother/infant dyads. In an address to the British Psychoanalytical Society, which contained the germ of much of his thinking, Winnicott says:

> I shall not first give an historical survey and show the development
> of my ideas from the theories of others, because my mind does not
> work that way. What happens is that I gather this and that, here and
> there, settle down to clinical experience, form my own theories and
> then, last of all interest myself in looking to see where I stole what.
> Perhaps this is as good a method as any. (Winnicott, 1945, p. 145)

Although he considered his work to be a logical extension of that of Freud and Klein, Winnicott's aim in positioning himself in psychoanalytic thought was the same as for his patients. He was determined to be himself and not simply to conform. "The interplay between originality and the acceptance of tradition as the basis for inventiveness seems to me to be just one more example, and a very exciting one, of the interplay between separateness and union" (Winnicott, 1967b, p. 134).

In a letter to Harry Guntrip, Winnicott said that "any theories that I may have which are original are only valuable as a growth of ordinary Freudian psycho-analytic theory" (Rodman, 1999, p. 75). But he both did and did not think his work was in continuity with Freud's (Goldman, 1993). Later, he privately told Guntrip that "we disagree with Freud [...] He was for airing symptoms. We are concerned with whole living and loving persons" (cited in Mendez & Fine, 1976, p. 361). His objective was different from but based on Freud's. Winnicott, as he got older became interested in enjoyment and health. He stressed the importance of those quiet special yet enjoyable experiences that go to making a full life. He emphasised the quality indicators of creative living, wellbeing, aliveness, spontaneity, and feeling real, where Freud stressed instincts and the basal indicators of freedom from disease. It is from this that we get Winnicott's saying that "We are poor indeed if we are only sane" (1945, p. 150). Winnicott said that "Freud was easy to criticise because he was always critical of himself" (1962a, p. 177).

Of Klein, Winnicott says: "I believe my views began to separate out from hers, and in any case I found that she had not included me in as a Kleinian" (p. 177). Winnicott speaks at length of what he gained from Klein. He believed that there was, in his supervision with her, a strict adherence to Freudian principals of technique with care taken to remain within the analyst's role and an emphasis on transference interpretations. Her influence is obvious throughout the pages of the published transcript of Winnicott's fragment of "The Case of Boredom" (1989).

Winnicott (1962a) was grateful to Klein for the following introductions: to the concept of pregenital anxieties; to the technique of play; to the internal world of the infant; to the ability to localise the item of psychic reality inside or outside; to projection and introjection. He also felt that the idea that changes came about from eating, that is, oral eroticism and sadism, was important. He considered the depressive position to be a badly named good idea. Reparation, he believed, was Klein's most important contribution, providing an explanation of how the child comes to feel guilt.

Amongst Klein's more questionable contributions in Winnicott's (1962a) mind was the tendency, in her later theory, to push the age at which mental mechanisms appear further back and also what he called her "lip-service" to environmental provision. Her doubtful notions in his view included retaining a use for the theory of the life and death instincts. He also questioned the usefulness of what he saw as her attempt to "restate infantile destructiveness" in terms of heredity and envy. The situation at the beginning with the baby and the breast is one of identity for Winnicott and this precludes the possibility of envy. At the beginning for Freud there is pleasure seeking, for Klein there is object relating, and for Winnicott there is dependence.

Winnicott's roots in the general area of child development research

There were, however, other trends in psychoanalysis at that time that may be seen as having influenced Winnicott's reliance on the interaction between the mother and baby for his model of mind and of the analytic process. Let us briefly consider some of these: Bion (1955, 1961) also gave emphasis to the model of a mother–baby interaction. His concept of the mother's reverie is similar to Winnicott's notion of the mother's holding function in general and primary maternal preoccupation in particular. Balint (1935, 1968) worked contemporaneously but independently of Winnicott and, like him, saw regression in analysis as curative and strengthening of the ego. The patient goes back, pre-trauma, to heal the wounds to the ego, as Winnicott says, or to mourn its losses, in Balint's construction.

Freud did not engage in the analysis of children; he relied on the observations of his own children or on the observations of friends or colleagues to check his theory of childhood *in vivo*. Hence he used the notes taken by the actual father for his analysis of Little Hans. Hug-Hellmuth (1921) and others considered that the psychoanalysis of children was best conducted through education. Her attitude is reflected also in Anna Freud's claim that the child cannot be launched into the analysis as the adult is and needs a "warming up" period of preparation and guidance.

By attributing central importance to the Oedipus complex, Winnicott (1954) thinks that Freud failed to account for the many people who have not reached that stage. He feels that in his self analysis and with his patient group, Freud could presume a good enough environment. He therefore saw little difficulty arising from this stage and considered its curative element to be unimportant.

In 1924, however, Freud wrote to Ferenczi who believed that the analyst should behave like an affectionate mother, saying that there might be something in his two-person psychology for which he, Freud, was not yet ready (cited in van Sweden, 1995). This correspondence with a person who might be regarded as the father (and by some as the misguided father) of two-person psychology, can be read as Freud's blessing to those for whom the area of interest in early development lies before the Oedipus complex.

Freud's daughter, Anna, was involved, for example, in the Bulldog Banks studies of orphans of the Second World War. These studies were part of a greater global interest in the general area of infant research and child development theory in the 1930s and 1940s which comprised part of a post-war response. These studies, completed by such notable figures as John Bowlby, examined the impact of maternal deprivation, separation, and the early experience generally on subsequent mental health and social adjustment (cited in Davenport, 1994). This was mirrored by a simultaneous growth in the area of child analysis. It was in this child-focused environment that Winnicott worked.

Summary

In this chapter, I have explored the views of both Freud and Klein on early experience and I have briefly traced the movement to object relating and the mother's influence on development. This enables an exploration of the contribution to Winnicott's thinking, providing evidence for continuities with Winnicott's work in the subsequent chapters. It was with the same purpose that we briefly visited the wave of interest in child development in which Winnicott found himself working.

CHAPTER TWO

Absolute dependence: the growth of a boundary

The following two chapters illuminate the early time between autoeroticism and the Oedipus complex. In this chapter, I illustrate the clinical usefulness of this understanding, looking at the very beginning of life and the stage that Winnicott called "absolute dependence" or "double dependence".

Kenneth Wright says that "Separating out has two main aspects—the growth of a boundary, and the development of distance between self and other" (1991, p. 60). In broad terms, this chapter deals with the growth of a boundary, and in the next chapter I treat the "distance between". Here, I look at the parallels between the nursing and analytic couples. I focus on the nature of absolute dependence by examining the important concepts, attaching it to Winnicott's thinking, and their function in the first developmental situation pertaining with the infant, and then in the analytic situation involving adult patients. In this chapter, and the two chapters that follow, this is done by referencing examples—all fictionalised and of a composite nature—from an eighteen-month-long infant observation completed by the author (which can be read in full in Chapter Five) and from clinical vignettes from the author's adult caseload.

Winnicott's idea of human nature and human development has been noted for its optimism and for its emphasis on health. At the beginning, for Winnicott there is inherited potential and a tendency towards health. There is a propensity for mature functioning and creative living. In short, there is a maturational sequence, which can unfold naturally in the good enough environment of the "ordinary devoted" care of the mother.

Winnicott gives much of his attention, and a primacy of importance, to the ego rather than the instinct. The ego is there at the beginning as potential. It is in an unintegrated state and for that reason needs the holding and facilitating environment of the mother. For Winnicott, between autoeroticism and the recognition of the object as whole and separate, comes his idea of this transitional space that first arises between the mother and the baby and which is the prototype for all further healthy and enjoyable intrapsychic and interpersonal experience in the individual's future.

At the beginning there is no "me"/"not me" distinction. At birth, because there is no boundary there is no space and the infant has no means of knowing about the maternal care. The building of a space of experience depends on the building of a boundary and an ego. At the beginning, the baby's fragile ego can only begin to build when encased in the mother's reliable and stable care (the good enough environment). During this period the infant "cannot gain control over what is well and what is badly done, but is only in a position to gain profit or to suffer disturbance" (Winnicott, 1960a, p. 46). A very fundamental aspect of Winnicott's distinctive vision lies in the way he conceptualises birth. He saw that the physical birth and separation of the infant from the mother was also, in fact, his psychical entry into unity with her, with self and surroundings undistinguished. Subjective birth is a later and more gradual achievement.

Developing a sense of self is an aim which the processes of maturation and analysis have in common. It seems that the main developmental task of this stage of absolute dependence is achieved when a rudimentary boundary is established between self and other, which Winnicott calls "unit status". An objective understanding of the nature of "other" and the "distance" or "space between" is for the next stage of dependence—"relative dependence".

It is important to note here that it is not the physical dependence on the mother for survival that is at issue. Winnicott emphasises rather the baby's absolute dependence on the mother for the meeting of ego needs—for example, for the experience of self through the other while being fed.

I recognised this dependence in the mother/infant unit on my first visit to the newborn of my baby observation . There was, as Winnicott suggests, "no such thing as a baby". My first sight was of a "nursing couple", of the mother sitting up in her hospital bed holding her baby. And for the next eight visits, now at home, the baby was mostly in the mother's arms. On this first visit in the hospital, when the baby was one day old, the mother gave me the baby to hold so quickly that it had happened before I knew it but, as I settled to enjoy the situation, I could feel the quality of the baby's weight change in my arms as she fell asleep in the same way that one can sometimes feel the nature of a silence change in a session.

For Winnicott, the baby is not the psychologically discrete and viable unit at birth that he is considered to be in much psychoanalytic thinking. On the contrary there is between the mother and the infant, what he called the fact of dependence.

> ... before object relationships [...] the unit is not the individual, the unit is an environment-individual set-up [...] by good-enough child care [...] the shell becomes gradually taken over and the kernel (which has looked all the time like a human baby to us) can begin to be an individual. (Winnicott, 1952, p. 99)

The holding environment

For Winnicott, the experience the baby has of environmental provision determines whether life is enjoyed and lived creatively or felt to be a painful and somewhat pointless struggle. The mother acts as a boundary until the baby can do it for himself. Winnicott called the mother's provision of this environment "holding". Subsumed within holding are the sub-functions of "handling" and "object-presenting". These will be treated further in Chapter Three. For the present, suffice it to say that handling refers to the importance of the quality of the physical aspects of babycare and that object-presenting refers to the fact that the way the mother presents herself to the baby tells him about himself more than about her at this time of absolute dependence. Of the psychological and physical holding that an infant needs he "only understands love that is expressed in physical terms [...] by live human holding [...] we are more concerned with the mother holding the baby than the mother feeding the baby" (Winnicott, 1955, p. 191).

Although holding is crucial at the stage of absolute dependence, it goes beyond this stage. Its nature changes from the holding to which the boundariless baby is oblivious at the beginning, to the baby's recognition of the mother's holding, and continues to expand to take in first the mother, father, and baby living together and then an ever expanding environment in the good situation (Winnicott, 1960a).

The holding environment of the completely adapted and attuned mother protects the baby from what Winnicott calls "impingement". In his unintegrated state, the baby would suffer trauma if he were required to react to his environment rather than have his environment adapt to him. There are two possible sources of impingement or trauma against which the mother's psychical and physical holding protect the baby.

The first is against having to react to external source. The thinking here can be confusing because Winnicott considers as "external" those internal sources which are experienced by the infant as external, such as pain and hunger. As mature adults, we consider these to be internal, but to the immature infant they are impinging events coming from outside and to which he or she must react.

I observed a good example of the mother holding the baby against the pain of colic at seven weeks old. The mother was at once able to use the knowledge which she drew from her unity with and her separateness from her baby. The mother's firm and comforting hold on the baby was the difference between distressed pain and annihilation. The mother could feel the baby's distress but she was also feeling sufficiently separate to remember in the midst of the baby's extreme distress that what the baby had was not life threatening.

The other source of impingement is the intensity of baby's own instinct, which the mother can help to regulate. At nine weeks the mother was concerned that the baby's extreme hunger and resulting strong and greedy gulping would result in stomach pain. The mother rocked the baby and she massaged the baby's back and stroked her hair so that, taking account of the rhythm of the mother's touch, the baby came out of the grip of her hungry greed and into a pace of feeding which was less frenetic and calmer.

The baby's perspective on the unit

Winnicott was able to envisage simultaneously the different perspectives of the immature baby and his mature mother. In this book, we do it by turns. In this section, I first take the opportunity to look at things from the baby's perspective, and then in the next section we focus on the mother's perspective on this first stage of the infant's life, when they are inextricably linked. Winnicott saw the real necessity of considering separately the infant's perspective, as it was of such a fundamentally different nature to that of the mature adult.

At this time, when there is no fundamental "me/not me" boundary, the baby has no sense of agency. He has no sense of being able to stop things or make things happen. In the hospital, on the baby's first day, she would latch on to the breast and then, having lost the breast, continue to make loud smacking and sucking noises, unable to tell the difference between the mouth and the breast. In Winnicott's thinking, when the child is held in stillness and adapted to, so that he does not have to react or go without, experience builds on experience, enhancing his sense of himself and his confidence that what he needs he will "create/get". Primary creativity, or what Erikson (1950) calls "basic trust", develops here, where inside and outside do not exist. It develops if the baby can experience reliability over time.

In the observation, when the baby tucked her knees up and cried, the mother moved her to ease her discomfort. She kept painful sensations within tolerable limits for the baby. The baby's eyes remained closed but her facial expression showed her reactions to the tactile and proprioceptive sensations. This primary creativity, the fact of getting/ creating what he wants (in other words feeling like God) will allow him to weather frustration later when the division is achieved and the boundary exists. Most importantly, it will enable him to forge links between his inner and outer realities, because the baby will trust that in the real world he will find what he needs.

For Winnicott, the baby at this stage "is" according to the style, pace, mood, manner, and atmosphere that is intrinsic to the mother's "way of being herself", as well as according to her way of looking after her baby. It is from all of this that the qualitative shape of this developing "self" evolves. It is the constancy in the mother's always being "herself"; even, predictable, and adaptive to the baby, she is experienced over time in a way that allows the baby to come into being and the boundary to develop. This entire process cannot be recognised or articulated in any way. Happening at a time preceding the recognition of the need for words, it has no alternative or comparison. This is for Winnicott "being", or the "female element", and it develops in the baby's personality in the stage of absolute dependence. It is related to the love instinct and the "environment mother", that is, the mother of babycare. "Being" must be established before "doing"; the "male element" of the personality can be later established. It is the constancy of the mother in her way of being herself and the constancy of her reliable care, along with the baby's experience of primary creativity, which allows him eventually to countenance his separateness and acknowledge the full range of his instinctual life without fear. "Being" is linked with the experience of unintegration and the capacity to be temporarily boundariless. "Being" is the early precursor of relaxation, of enjoyment, of playing, and of the capacity to live creatively. In his experience of "being" the breast and "being" the mother, the baby takes on the mother's entire way of being as an unspoken aspect of himself.

Winnicott puts trust in human nature and does not draw the pessimistic conclusions of Sartre (1957), for whom there is no possibility of real or rewarding relation to the other. For Sartre, one has either to relinquish one's subjectivity to that of the other or to objectify the other in order to maintain one's subjectivity. In contrast, Khan (1958) explains Winnicott's view of man as "an unknowable isolate who could [...] know himself only through the *other*" (p. xiv). From Winnicott's perspective, the subjectivity of the individual is only started off by virtue of this first good enough encounter with the other, through the other's willingness, and before the other is in any way recognised. The very best in enjoyable creative living and culture are extensions or vestiges of this encounter. Before experiencing himself as a separate self with a boundary, the baby becomes a person first in the mind and imaginative elaborations of the mother.

The observed baby had only to be born, to set in place the mother's response of complete adaptation. Here, this observed baby was "held" in mind as well as in the mother's physical embrace. The mother gave a special amount of her attention to the baby at all times in the first two months. In these early days, the mother spoke of her baby in positive superlatives. The baby was "perfect" in her eyes and she therefore wanted everything to be "perfect" for the baby.

For Winnicott, what makes the mother's holding function absolutely vital is the newborn's simultaneous obliviousness of and identification with the mother. He recognised that the mother's constancy and reliability in the care of her baby is the process by which the baby begins to integrate different aspects of himself, so that his self experience and boundary build and grow stronger. It is by her attention to the baby's ego needs and sensitivity to his self-experience that the baby knows that, whether fed and falling asleep or hungry and wracked with colicky pain, he is still the same person. By his mother's attention to his ego needs, the baby's potential unfolds, such that he begins to feel real and connects to the world. From the baby's perspective, there is a growth in his capacity to experience which he does not relate to the mother. Winnicott referred to this "process" experience of the mother function as the "environment mother". The "object mother" of feeding, and the baby's instinctual life, will be explored in the next chapter.

The mother's perspective on the unit

Winnicott's "primary maternal preoccupation" (1956) describes the state of mind in the months during and after pregnancy in which she is sensitive to the experience and needs of her baby. "Primary maternal preoccupation" allows the mother to provide adequate holding for her newborn; one has to be healthy to be sick in this way because what is involved is a temporary split in the ego.

In this regard, it was apparent to me that volunteering to take part in an infant observation was an attempt on the part of the observed baby's mother to build up the psychical space and uniqueness of her new baby even when it was still in utero. I know that she was thinking that part of this fourth baby's uniqueness was that it would be a "lone" baby. The others, all boys, were born in quick succession. But this woman was tired in this pregnancy and her willingness to be involved in the baby observation seemed to be a way of defending against the limits of her own enthusiasm and also against the possible disappointment if this baby was another boy. From discussions we had, I know that this mother spent time thinking of and preparing for her baby and monitoring the other family members' reaction to the news.

Winnicott was aware of the importance of the mother's capacity to attach meaning to the baby's existence at the beginning of life before he has the apparatus to process the experience himself. However, it is important that her response is not to a fantasised baby, but to the real live one. The temporary split in the mother's ego is an accommodation to the baby's need for the mother to create an illusion and respond as though they were one, whilst simultaneously recognising their separateness. In the early days, the observation mother spent much time, while feeding the baby, admiring and fondling her, relating her to others and speculating as to what she would become. These possibilities were first conceived in the mother's imaginative elaborations, just as the physical reality of the baby first grew in her body.

The good enough mother makes good use of her own boundary and does not identify fully with the baby. Winnicott says that the richness of experience is "built on monotony" and that the part of the mother remaining outside the unity, her ability to continue being herself, allows her to be constant and even in her handling of the baby. This gives the baby a continuity of impingement-free experience that allows him to "be".

In the good enough situation, earliest communication involves the mother and the baby transmitting feeling states to each other, that is, silent communication. This was very evident when, in the infant observation, the mother and the baby mirrored each other's rare desultory moods. It provided ample proof, also, that the feeling states that are transmitted are not always positive. The absolutely dependent baby makes demands such that they engender hate as well as love. The good enough mother acknowledges and expresses these feelings in a way which still meets the baby's ego needs. Winnicott (1968) gives the example of the baby burbling at the violent content of the lullaby "Hush-a-bye, baby, on the tree tops", once mother sings it pleasantly.

When the observation baby was six weeks old, the mother said "It's great when you get to know them". She felt confident that she knew what her baby needed and this in turn made her feel good. During the observation this mother anticipated her baby's hunger and wind so that painful episodes were avoided for the baby, and her mother was given the pleasure of guessing correctly. The feelings that the baby put into the mother were not always positive ones, however. This mother was aware of her own feelings of annoyance at the baby for screaming and scratching at her breast, and also on those occasions when she had to clean up the baby's sick. She said things which acknowledged her anger and resentment at the bother of baby care, but in a tone of voice that did not in any way traumatise the baby.

As we shall see in Chapter Three, according to Winnicott (1967b), we live and keep our ideas of what he calls "self" in the third area of experience. The other two areas of inside (me) and outside (not me) meet in this "third" or "between" area which is contributed to by both. In this "between" area, we keep our idea of self, past, present, and future. Now in the pre-boundary state, the mother holds the ideas of self for the baby. She holds the wonder and importance attaching to the birth for herself and her unaware newborn. In the good situation, as above, the mother balances her excited care of her newborn with a protective respect and acknowledgement of this new, separate selfhood. She holds and shares in the baby's early experience so that his capacity to "live" or "feel" an experience grows and his ego strengthens and boundary develops. In time he will not need this "auxiliary ego".

The mother provides this "continuity-of-being" in a conscious way also, later bolstering the child's sense of self by sharing her memories of how things were, her mixture of feelings then, etc. These memories confirm in consciousness the "aesthetic of being", laid down in the baby's self by the mother's early handling of him. This function seems to be served all through a child's life and may account for the special loss of self felt for example, by an only child on the death of his parents. Who else knows the person's story from the very beginning and in such detail? It must seem in an intense way that the knowledge reservoir of one's self is gone, as is the original mould for a way of living and seeing the world.

Analytical setting as the technical equivalent of mother's holding

Winnicott considered the concept of "analytic setting" to be of great importance. In the next two sections, we look first at the relationship of the concept of analytical setting to the mother/infant unit, and then at the effects of a deficient environment at the beginning of life on subsequent adult analysis.

Whenever the content of the therapy relates to issues of the very early infant–mother relationship, the "analytic setting" is the most important feature of the analysis. For Winnicott, the psychoanalytic setting corresponds to the mother's holding function at this stage of absolute dependence (1971a). (Sometimes, as we shall see, it corresponds to her function in the next stage of relative dependence.) It is often the setting which provides the psychical and physical holding of the patient.

All the concepts attaching to this early stage, the mother–infant unit, holding, being, and primary maternal preoccupation, make up the setting. It refers to the reliability and constancy in the physical environment, the time and place in which the analysis occurs; importantly, it also refers to the therapist's attitude to the patient and the way that the therapist holds the patient in mind. Setting is to analysis what the mother's way of doing things is to infant care.

Freud's recommendations for the analytic setting aim to create optimal conditions for the development of the transference so that dynamics from the genetic situation and (from Freud's perspective) the mostly Oedipal situation would develop. Winnicott says, however, that Freud was unconsciously deferential to the importance of the first dyad in his recommendations for setting. He suggests that in effect what Freud recommended was the setting up of a good enough environment in the analytic situation.

In this way, one can see that the couch, the room, its contents and features, the beginning and ending times, and the regularity, are all preverbal symbols of the unity between the mother and the baby. Each symbolises the mother's care and love. As with the baby, Winnicott tells us that love is only understood when expressed in physical human holding; physiology has not separated from psychology. In the setting the patient experiences the analyst's reliability, sameness, and live interest. Giovacchini (1990b) describes a teenage self-destructive boy who was being treated in a residential setting. This boy was required to attend therapy, and he lay for four months of his sessions in the foetal position in front of a stove without in any way acknowledging the therapist. Giovacchini tells how this boy gradually began to come voluntarily to sessions and eventually acknowledged the therapist. He points to the physical aspects of the setting which first held the patient and facilitated him eventually to come to the point when it had felt safe enough—experienced over a sufficiently long period—to begin to talk to the therapist.

Winnicott states that the provision of an ordinary environment is more important than interpretation for a psychotic patient—that is, for someone who has issues relating to his boundary. He says that "For the neurotic the couch and warmth and comfort can be *symbolical* of the mother's love; for the psychotic it would be more true to say that these things *are* the analyst's physical expression of love" (Winnicott, 1947, p. 199, author's emphasis).

Winnicott broke the technique of analysis into two parts: interpretation and setting. Setting is paramount (1954). Firstly, the patient needs the experience of being held in unity, in an unintegrated state, and to feel the real therapist's adaptation and reliability over time. It is only on this foundation of holding that interpretation becomes useful.

In the next section, I consider the infant's state at birth without boundary or space, and I explore the implications of this state for therapy.

The patient's perspective

By now it is apparent that, for Winnicott, the baby's "me/not me" boundary builds by virtue of the mother's initial complete adaptation to the baby. It is the mother's complete and sensitive adaptation at the beginning that allows a sense of self to develop without dissociation or bits of the self splitting off and without a withdrawal into inner reality, in what Winnicott calls "fantasying" (1935, 1971b). Fantasying is a maladaptive version of dreaming which does not contribute anything to creative living. It is a dreaming that substitutes for creative living instead of enriching it. In the good situation, the holding environment is invisible and unnoticed but nonetheless crucial at this time when the baby can have no concept whatsoever of an environment or of an object. The importance of a "good enough environment" is really only borne out and apparent through the negative effect of its absence. Winnicott explains that with failure at the beginning of life "the infant cannot start the development that is born with him" (1962b). The earlier the failure of the environment to provide for the ego needs of the baby the greater the damage. There is a continuum of effect and environmental failure may result, for example, in childhood schizophrenia whereas a failure at a later stage may result in affective disorder or antisocial tendency, and later still in pathological dependence. At this early time in the deficient environment, the baby will suffer what Winnicott calls primitive agonies or unthinkable anxiety. These reflect the tactile and proprioceptive nature of the baby's earliest experience before sight, that is, going to pieces, falling forever, having no relation to the body or orientation, and complete isolation without any means of communication (Winnicott, 1962c, 1968). The mother's physical and psychical holding protects the baby from the sense of chaos and disintegration caused by these anxieties. The lasting effect of a collapse of the holding environment and the unbearable boundarilessness at this early stage is often in evidence in the analytic situation.

One patient regularly asks herself why her mother had her. She tells herself it was her mother's futile attempt to keep her relationship with the patient's father alive. Whereas the observation baby was good and welcome, the patient had no intrinsic value. The mother saw her as an ineffective "glue" with which she had hoped to fix the father's attachment to herself. There was no making of psychical space, no reverie, no primary maternal pre-occupation, no adaptation to or identification with baby's needs. Another patient's sick mother claims that she and her daughter are "as one" and the patient feels she will only be free to have her own life when her mother is dead. For both, the sense of self is severely impoverished by the feeling that this "reservoir of the self" never existed.

Another patient's recurrently expressed wish is for the experience she did not have of being held in her mother's arms and, by this experience, to be able to bear the traumata of her life. This is what she has wished for in her worst moments. She is haunted by painful memories from the past and an image of two photographs side by side. One is of her holding her own child as a baby. The other is of her mother holding her as a baby. What is pain-ful to her is the difference in the two photographs. Her oblivious mother is holding her as a newborn, dangling precariously like a rag-doll away from her body. Her mother's gaze and attention is going to the person taking the photograph, her father. When the patient was photographed with her own baby, she cradled him closely, remembering every detail of him and of her feelings for him and she looked at him lovingly for the photograph.

The patient says repeatedly that she has never been a child. Now she says she has never been a baby. The thought comes to the therapist that this is a new explanation of the patient's use of the couch. The patient agrees, explaining her habitual stance in sessions of sitting bolt upright on the edge of the couch. Trusting the situation enough to take up the typical position of a baby on the couch feels like a new and risky business for which she is not ready but which she now considers to be a valuable possibility for the future. She realises that what she fears is the experience of being "dropped". Winnicott alerts us to the crucial importance of the mother's complete adap-tation to the baby at the beginning so that the baby can "be".

A patient realised that growing up, and in adult life, she had never had the opportunity or entitlement to just "do nothing" and relax. For the first time she saw the value of time spent that way. The patient relates this to her feeling of dread on waking each morning. At the end of the day she earns retrospective entitlement to her life by what she has done, before start-ing over. The tidiness of her house is a measure of her worth as a person. The responsibility is endless. She does not feel "at home" at home. The only chance of relaxation is to go out. She must accommodate to the day and to the house. The idea that either might be modeled to serve her requirements for comfort or relaxation, strikes her as sensible but she cannot relate to it. This woman has not had the experience of being reliably and sensitively held so that she could just "be". She does not have that relation to her days or to her house. She cannot feel comfortably "held" in the house or in the environment of each new day. She reacts by "doing" in hope of warding off the feelings of annihilation or the expectation of harsh handling. This was even the patient's preoccupation in the session dealing with the very subject. The therapist had found the session to be "overpacked" but the patient, in uncharacteristically bouyant mood, described it as "productive".

The patient's pain in relation to "being", comes from what Winnicott calls a "fear of a breakdown" that has already happened but which cannot be felt (1963a). Something happened at the stage of absolute dependence, interfering with the baby's contented identification with the environment mother and feelings of primary creativity. This explains my patient's painful feelings in the present. Her "doing" attempts to ward off primitive anxiety which originated with the impingement close to the beginning of life.

For Winnicott, the result of deficiencies at the stage of "being" are worse than death. If the immature baby experiences the mother's separateness and boundary there is unbearable fragmentation and primitive agony.

A patient tells of a thought she had that frightened her. Lying face down on her bed, she wished that someone would come along and shoot her in the back of the head. One part of her self is frightened by another. She is afraid of how pleased she was with the thought, how right and good it seemed.

It seems that even the wish for death can be an attempt to discover, or recover, the feeling of oneness at the very beginning. The hopelessness around the wish for merger with mother, an experience which the patient has always needed, never got, and which one part of her despairs of, forms itself as a wish to merge in death into oneness and oblivion in the symbolic environment of bed. It is as though she expects to rest and "be", held safe in death in a way that is precluded in her daily way of being by the experience of the early environment.

Winnicott accounts for Freud's death drive in terms of failure of the environment at the earliest stage of absolute dependence, before "unit status" (1969). He said that if Freud had known what the treatment of schizophrenic and borderline patients had taught us since his death, he would not have posited the death drive. In this example, the self-destructive part of the patient relates to environmental deficiencies at the very beginning of her life which leave her with such feelings of rage and painful emptiness that death seems alarmingly preferable at times.

The analyst's perspective

Winnicott was wary of sentimentality in relation to babies because it involved the unhealthy denial of negative feelings, and also because it is dangerous if such feelings towards the nuisance of absolute dependence are denied in the analytic situation. The therapist is there to hold the environment of the analytic setting intact by sharing in the fantasy of unity but remaining also separate, making the split of primary maternal preoccupation so that the mother/baby unit can happen in the transference.

The first step in coming to this formulation was the therapist's acknowledgement of her own fantasy of this insatiable baby (who would remain with her into great age, seeing off her real children), and the naming to herself of her feelings of burden, resentment, and impossibility, which reflected those of the patient. The patient was not a baby but was ruthless like a baby in her attempt to get what she needed—the total adaptation which she had needed (and in a way still needed) in absolute dependence. Then the therapist could make the split of primary maternal preoccupation necessary to be part of the mother/baby unit of the transference. She could share the fantasy of unity but also remain separate, holding the environment of the analytic setting intact.

At the next session, the therapist delayed opening the door to the patient, by at most two seconds of real time. There was a noticeable delay in the patient's starting to speak her material and the therapist suggested that this might have to do with the delay in opening the door. "No, I know you were just keeping your work and family life separate", was the reply. But then the patient sobbed without knowing why. She felt excluded and hurt. Her fantasy of unity with the therapist jarred painfully with this piece of reality which made it clear that she was in fact a separate individual who featured in the professional rather than personal life of the therapist.

From Winnicott's perspective, it is understandable that such an encounter might be felt as the therapist's hate, in the same way as Winnicott says the ending of the session may be experienced as the analyst's hate. This is the transitional space of analysis. The therapist did wake early thinking of the patient. So it is at the same time true and untrue to say that the patient is only a feature of the therapist's working day. At the stage of absolute dependence in the therapy, it is important that the therapist holds the feelings and uses them to understand the patient. It is understandable at this stage, which Winnicott (1952) calls "pre-ruth", that the patient does not acknowledge feelings of hate or love or even the personhood of the therapist. Winnicott seldom spoke of transference or countertransference but warned of the extra strain there is in working with psychotics or people who have not achieved "unit status". It is important for the therapist to be able to admit to feelings equivalent to those experienced by the mother through primary maternal preoccupation.

Giovacchini (1990a) speaks of this temporary split of the ego as a useful stance for the therapist in the treatment of adults with ego deficits or boundary issues. He outlines its effectiveness in his treatment of an adult patient whose reasons for wanting him to be responsible for her life and therapy he could and could not understand and agree with. Giovacchini calls this split "not quite absolute dependence". It is similar in nature to the split made with the above patient who was in the impossible position of wanting and not wanting therapy. It was this understanding which alleviated the impossibility of the situation for the therapist.

Summary

I have considered the infant's state at birth without boundary or space and then looked at the implications for therapy that arise out of this. I have shown how the baby feels completely identified with the mother at the very beginning of life—and needs to experience this. We have seen here too how, by virtue of primary maternal preoccupation, the mother adapts to her baby's needs and the baby's self begins in her imaginings.

In the maturational model, these things are accounted for by Winnicott's concepts of being, holding, primary preoccupation, and silent communication. In the translation of these concepts to the analytic situation, we have seen how they are subsumed in the concept of analytical setting—that is, in both its physical aspect and in the person of the therapist. The reliable care of the "ordinary devoted mother" in either the developmental first or in the analytic setting must be experienced over time. Then, with an emergent boundary, the foundation is set for the transitional space to develop and a readiness for the beginnings of a gradual move away from absolute dependence.

CHAPTER THREE

Relative dependence: the distance between

ecall the beginning of the last chapter, where I quoted Kenneth Wright, who says: "Separating out has two main aspects—the growth of a boundary, and the development of distance between self and other" (1991, p. 60). We have dealt in the last chapter with the growth of a boundary, so we are now ready to examine the nature of the developing "distance between". Again, we do this by looking at the parallels between the nursing and the analytic couples.

In the previous chapter, by virtue of the mother's good enough holding, we have seen how the rudimentary boundary between the "me" and the "not me" begins to emerge during the stage of absolute dependence. In this chapter, I look at the stage of relative dependence, where this boundary from the last stage is strengthened, and how the third area or space between the nursing couple is established. First, I look at the concepts relating to transitional phenomena by which the baby emerges from unity with the mother and manages the interaction of his inner and outer reality. Next, I examine the baby's maturational changes. These integrate his idea of the mother, making him aware of his indebtedness, and allowing the development of the transitional space—the "distance between" in which experience builds and the nature of the other is appreciated. I visit the changing mother function with a section on each of her three tasks: holding, object-presenting, and handling. Here, the mother completes the necessary disillusionment whilst presenting himself, herself, and the world to the baby in "managed and manageable" doses. Finally, I look at this stage in the analytic space. I look at the evidence for transitional phenomena before exploring the implications of deficits in environmental provision at this stage, first for the patient's growth, and then for the analyst's function.

Transitional phenomena

Winnicott (1951, 1953) worked throughout his career on these enduring concepts of transitional phenomena which Anna Freud told him had "conquered the analytic world" (Rodman, 1987). Transitional phenomena are the first step in the journey from unaware absolute dependence and take place in "the intermediate area of experience between the thumb and the teddy bear; between oral eroticism and the true object-relationship" (Winnicott, 1953, p. 2). The child develops his sense of self and experiences the co-existence of separation and unity. The child balances feeling real, alive, and autonomous with feeling connected and related in his experience. He lives between dependence and independence, fantasy and reality, conception and perception. This capacity develops over time and is, ultimately, internalised as the "good enough" environment, as we will see in Chapter Four.

For Winnicott, this area of experience is "a resting place" from "the perpetual human task of keeping inner reality and external life separate yet interrelated". It is an illusion that is allowed to the infant and which, throughout life, is the basis of all social, aesthetic, spiritual, and cultural life. In transitional space we find a balance between fact and fantasy in our intrapsychic experience, and in the interpersonal experience between individuality and relatedness. It is for this reason that this stage of relative dependence is the stage of transitional space per se. It may be viewed as the space that represents the essential nature of the human condition and of meaningful human experience (Winnicott, 1967b).

In the rest of this section, I show the basis of transitional phenomena, both in the concept of potential space and in Winnicott's explanation of the experience of time elapsing. I show how the baby, once he has found the first boundary of his skin, finds transitional objects, and in this way can eventually play and interact with his environment.

Transitional phenomena are based on Winnicott's concept of potential space. Potential space is a paradoxical space which joins and separates the mother and her baby and arises at the end of the stage of being merged when the rudimentary boundary has formed. Its basis is the *trust* that the baby has from experiencing the reliability of the mother over a long enough time at a critical phase of the separation of the "not-me" from the "me" (Winnicott, 1971c). It is characterised by freedom for variability. One is not fixed in potential space, which is the area of all possible selves, of all possible worlds, of all possible lives. It is because of the effect and the variability of one's experiences in this potential space that the environment has such importance for Winnicott. In the facilitating situation, the separateness/unity paradox spans from the first relationship, up to the pontential space which connects and separates the individual from a rich and meaningful life in all its spheres.

Winnicott uses the letters x, y, and z to denote amounts of time when speaking of transitional space. There is a magical unreal quality to the x time of absolute dependence. In x time, the mother is completely and instantaneously adaptive to the baby so that he feels he creates what he needs. He wants the breast and it is there. He has the experience that what he wants arrives by virtue of his thinking that he wants it. Transitional space is the space of $x + y$ time. By contrast with the immediate gratification of absolute dependence, it involves an amount of waiting or separateness which enhances the sense of self, making one feel more real. It is the meaningful experience which comes after x, the meaninglessness of hallucination and perfect magical adaptation on the one hand, and before the trauma of $x + y + z$ time, on the other. In $x + y + z$ time, the impact of the experience of separation or waiting is more than can be borne without a break in the continuity-of-being. It results in disintegration, chaos, and psychotic anxiety, which in turn lead to conformity, unreality, narcissistic, schizoid, or dissociative states (1967b).

The first and fundamental boundary separating the baby from the outside world is his skin. It holds him and all his bits intact. As will be demonstrated in examples, the mother's three tasks of holding, handling, and object-presenting let the baby feel himself as a finite being having achieved "unit status". In this way the mother helps her baby through the three maturational processes, that is, the way he experiences himself taking up time and space in the world (realisation), the way he inhabits his body (personalisation), and integrates his experiences (integration). It is on the basis of this boundary that transitional space now begins to build.

The transitional object is "one of the bridges that make contact possible between the individual psyche and external reality" (Winnicott, 1955, p. 149). Winnicott observed that when the baby is between four and eight months old, for example, a cot-sheet is introduced to complicate an oral autoerotic activity. It takes on an importance like a "me extension" for the infant that the parents intuitively respect (1951, 1953). The object, word, or mannerism is used to defend against anxiety, particularly depressive anxiety, which is the fear of the loss of the mother/breast. This important sequence of events "starts with the newborn infant's fist-in-mouth activities and leads eventually to an attachment" (Winnicott, 1953, p. 2).

By the time she was twelve weeks, the baby I observed had many transitional objects. She used her thumb and sometimes her fingers to soothe herself. The mother introduced a soother which the baby accepted readily. Later, each time her white blanket was put over her, she became calm and turned her attention to sleep. This allowed the mother more freedom of movement around the house and made the experience of the adequate provision perfect. The transitional object is the baby's first possession, his first use of a symbol, and his first experience of play. It is a "symbol of the union of the baby and the mother" and is as important for being real in itself as it is for symbolising the mother. It is *found* by the baby and yet in its significance *created* by him. The use of transitional objects indicates health (Winnicott, 1960b).

Freud (1920) explained an eighteen month old boy's *"fort-da"* ("gone-there") game, when he repeatedly threw away and retrieved a reel on a piece of string, in terms of anxiety management through symbol-formation and the active re-enactment of and mastery over a separation from his mother that he had already endured. For Winnicott, it is about the use of the transitional space. In an interesting remark, he noted the use of string, where separateness is at once recognised and denied in the string's communicative and binding functions respectively. He noted exaggerated use of the object when separation threatened. The object is kept significant or alive only by the availability and care of the actual mother. It cannot substitute for the mother, but makes adequate adaptation perfect and helps the integrating process of the ego. Its fate is that it is "relegated to limbo". It loses meaning when in health its significance is diffused over the "whole cultural field". It is obsolete when the growing child can, through ego strength, keep inside and outside apart and yet interrelated.

Having learned to extend himself into the mother and the outside world through the use of transitional objects, the baby can now also relate parts of his internal world to things in the real world through playing (Winnicott, 1942). Playing is evidence of a transitional space and of a boundary. It is a bridging of inside and outside. The quality of playing indicates the player's sense of self. It may be an enjoyable dramatisation of the inner world or an anxious, compulsive denial of it. It is communication and a way of processing self-experience. There is magic in the intimacy with which the baby experiences the mother's empathy, communication, mutuality, and reliability. There is excitement in the "interplay of the personal psychic reality and the experience of control of actual objects" (Winnicott, 1971c). Winnicott (1996, 1941) first used the notion of playing, clinically, in the diagnostic tools of the squiggle and spatula games before generalising its application to all human experience.

The area of play for the sensitively managed child is immense. In one of the later observation visits, the mother suggested that the box of baby wipes was a drum by tapping on it. The baby took up this meaning and both enjoyed taking turns. Then the baby, changing the subject, introduced the mother's second hand and a "to and fro" rather than "up and down" movement to make the box into a piano and the mother said "Oh, you have me playing the piano like Daddy". Because of her experiences with the mother, as taken-for-granted reality ground, the baby could now share a play area between them with the mother as a whole and separate person. When a child enjoys playing, there is a "seamless" quality to the experience, and he is unaware of what comes from inside or outside. It is similar for the adult with meaningful and enjoyable experience when one must stop and think to say whether something originated in ones inner reality or elsewhere. This seamlessness is the vestige of primary creativity.

Of the four stages referred to by Winnicott (1971c) in the development of playing, the above example of the baby's playing belongs to the last stage. The foundation for playing is the capacity of the baby to be "alone in the presence of someone" because the mother loves her reliably and is still there even after the baby has temporarily forgotten her. This means that the baby is now able to share a play area between them with tolerance of ideas not her own. A predominance of the fourth stage marks the movement "towards independence", as we will see in Chapter Four. In general terms, there is a move away from the subjective object of absolute dependence, towards a whole and separate objective object.

The baby's growth in relative dependence

The stage of relative dependence proceeds only on the basis that the stage of absolute dependence has gone well. Now with a boundary, the baby realises that he is dependent: "Here the infant can become aware of the need for the details of maternal care, and can to a growing extent relate them to personal impulse" (Winnicott, 1960a, p. 46). This is the stage of the baby's transition from being merged with or creating his mother, to loving and being loved by her as a whole and separate person to whom he is indebted, who is like him in some ways and not in others.

In the baby's physiological development, *sight* is as important as the proprioceptive and tactile sensations in the previous stage. In the case of the baby I observed, recognition of the boundaries of the observation visits grew from oblivion, to a registering of my face as a new feature. Next there were varying welcome reactions to my arrival, right up to the point when she started to play with the visit's boundaries. She explored my face and other features. Then there were the physical boundaries: running, hiding, peeping, coming behind me, patting my back, and putting things into my hands to hold, which she later retrieved.

In relative dependence, the baby "knows in his mind" that he depends on the mother. His perceptual and cognitive advances mean that he comes to see the mother as a whole and separate object. The eight-month-old baby can "hold" the whole mother in "view" so that space can separate and connect them. The baby sees that the environment mother of babycare and ego needs is also the object mother of instinctual urge who has survived his greedy feeding attacks when he destroyed her in phantasy over and over again. Now the baby can use memory and mental representations to keep the image of the mother alive and allow him to wait. He starts to use thinking as a kind of mothering substitute or bridge spanning the gap between experiencing a need and the filling of that need. Winnicott says this of kitchen noises: "Instead of simply being excited by the noises, the infant uses the news item in order to be able to wait" (1963b, p. 87). During this stage, which lasts from six months to two years, the infant's need of the care of the actual mother may become "fierce and truly terrible" (Winnicott, 1963b). This growing awareness accounts for the new fretfulness that the baby showed during the observation, at the observer's arrival, or mother's leaving the room.

The infant's spontaneous gestures or "doing" have expanded by this stage of relative dependence which, as we have seen in Chapter Two, has the successful "being" of absolute dependence as its basis. Whereas "being" has to do with the "female element" and the love instinct, "doing" is related to the "male element" and the motility drive. It accounts for the baby's aliveness and for his assertion of his existence (in fantasy, the destruction of the "not me"). Now the baby becomes simultaneously aware of both the fact of his dependency and the fact that the environment mother of the quiet times and the object mother of the excited times are one and the same. The baby's concern for the mother whom he has destroyed in the unconscious fantasy attaching to feeding may limit his aliveness and spontaneity. This is not the case with the father, with whom the baby has never been merged. Here the father may serve a very vital role as the first whole separate, and for that reason, safe object with whom the baby can assert his "me-ness". At this time, the baby's concern for his mother may be held in the space between his father and himself. Winnicott (1963c) explains that at this stage, it is by her survival that the externality of the mother is realised for the baby. In the good situation, spontaneity is therefore maintained, as the baby's "doing" is received as "gifts" or restitutive gestures which are enjoyed and welcomed by the mother.

At this time, the baby shows an early capacity to identify—he smiles when being smiled at and puts his finger in the mother's mouth when she is feeding him, as though feeding her. It is by this ability to identify that he sidetracks the hatred engendered by the challenge to his experience of omnipotence which is happening at this time. It also helps the infant to the "guilt sense" and to the "stage of concern" (Winnicott's equivalent of Klein's depressive position). Time and time again, the baby feels guilt when he takes responsibility for his instinctual urge to feed. He feels the drive to possess and destroy the contents of the object mother whilst wishing to protect the environment mother. This explains his motivation in weaning. The anxiety thus generated is modified in the baby's growing confidence that he can contribute to the mother as well as take from her. "Held" anxiety becomes a "guilt sense", which is further modified into concern as ambivalence is achieved. All morality is based on the developmental achievement of the baby's capacity for *concern*, which is in turn dependent on the experience of the mother's survival and opportunities to contribute (Winnicott, 1963d).

The mother's function in relative dependence

In this stage the mother's three tasks—namely of holding, handling, and object- presenting—are just as important as they were in absolute dependence but have a different quality. With the rudimentary boundary formed, the mother helps the baby to keep inside and outside separate but related. In absolute dependence the mother's approach is based on her capacity to empathise with the baby. In the stage of relative dependence, on the other hand, at the times when the baby is merged, he still needs empathy, but when he is separate, he needs an understanding based on his signals. In the good enough situation, the mother will know from the baby which is required when and in what proportion.

I will first explore the changes in the mother's holding function in this stage. Here the mother has to provide for a sense of safety and confidence that comes from the fact that she holds the baby in mind. The care she provides is still reliable, but it is not based on the same total adaptation she showed in absolute dependence. In the infant observation, the mother had the steady and even approach which her baby needed. In the evening she would sit on the couch, sometimes with the baby in her arms and sometimes allowing her to explore nearby. The mother was always there and generally in good form. Although she also refereed minor disputes, took homework consultations, and listened to her childrens' requests and stories, she was always available to the baby.

As part of her holding function, the mother has also to allow her baby to experience formlessness, which Winnicott also called "moments of unintegration". In the reality ground of the mother's "present absence" or "absent presence", the child can let his desire build without intrusion. Winnicott called this time the "period of hesitation". In a set situation, he repeatedly observed the mother presenting her baby with a spatula. As a general principle, he found that the baby's need to let the desire for the spatula develop and be recognised in its own time is universal. Any attempts to have the baby take up the spatula before this moment results in distress. When the baby is allowed this period of hesitation, the result is confident, creative, and spontaneous play with the spatula. This initial experience of formlessness allows the child to play and spend moments absorbed in fantasy. It is the precursor of all creativity, enjoyable or relaxing experience, and the capacity to be immersed in work. It is the potential space of imaginative elaboration, neither inside nor outside, where the child plays, relaxes, enjoys himself, feels real, and which enhances his growing sense of self.

The third part of the holding function in this stage is the need for the mother to disillusion the baby, to "fail" him in relative terms, in order to enhance his sense of self. Winnicott's concept of failure (spelled with a small "f") happens in $x + y$ time. It is the healthy task of the mother who is still responsive to the baby's needs but now awaits his signal before she responds. The mother disillusions her baby due partly to her remembering herself and partly to her continuing to be herself. The disillusionment process allows the infant to feel his needs, his own effort to get what he wants and to feel "real". The immediate mending of the failure allows the baby to experience both the good maternal care, which is the usual feature, and the separateness of the self and object. If the mother cannot fail in this way, then Winnicott says she does something worse than castrating the baby. "The creative gesture, the cry, the protest, all the little signs … are missing, because the mother has already met the need" (Winnicott, 1960a, p. 51). The baby remains in regressed merger or totally rejects mother. In the baby observation mentioned above, when solids were introduced, the visits moved from the sitting-room to the kitchen—to the imperfect ordinariness of the household. "Baby, you'll have to wait" was often the mother's response to the baby's first cry. Here the failure to provide perfection or magical adaptation also meant that the baby was included in, and a more real member of, the family. The space created by the disillusionment was filled with another kind of connection which extended now to the whole family. Involved in her daily work, the mother was also made more real and not just summoned and therefore only existing according to the baby's need. For Winnicott,

> … a very subtle distinction [exists] between the mother's understanding of her infant's need based on empathy, and her change over to an understanding based on something in the infant or small child that indicates need. This is particularly difficult […] because

> [...] children vacillate between one state and the other; one minute
> they are merged with their mothers and require empathy, while the
> next they are separate from her. (Winnicott, 1960a, pp. 51–52)

It is by allowing the baby to express his needs through her holding that the mother first introduces the reality principle and welcomes his spontaneous gestures.

The second of the mother's three tasks is that of object-presenting, by which the mother tells the baby about himself. She does this by the way in which she presents herself to him, by her approach to him, and by showing him what his presence means to her. Winnicott says that in the good situation the mother's face is a mirror: "the mother is looking at the baby and *what she looks like is related to what she sees there*" (Winnicott, 1967a, p. 151, author's emphasis). At the stage of absolute dependence, the mother's presentation of herself was related to the unintegrated passive baby himself. Now she also tells him about himself by her reaction to the evidence of his existence and his actions in the world. Sometimes the baby needs the mother to present herself as merged and sometimes as separate. The good enough parent makes allowances at this time for the child's frail boundary and his difficulty in negotiating a space between inside and outside. Winnicott (1949) gives the example of the little girl who says she wants to fly. She is not told that this is nonsense but lifted up so that she can fly like a bird. The boundary between merger and separateness, inside and out, perception and conception, is ever-changing and delicate at this time, and the attuned mother allows for this.

The twelve-month-old baby I observed needed the mother to help her understand the concept of her own boundary when she played a particular game several times a day: she showed the mother something which she was considering eating. The mother's approval response meant "yes", "good", and the baby nodded gleefully and ate it. Her disapproval meant "bad", "yuck", "dirty", it stayed outside, and the baby laughed, shook her head, and discarded it. It was clear that the baby used the mother to form the concepts of what is appropriate to the baby's inside and what stays outside.

The good enough mother presents herself, taking account of how much separateness the baby can manage at any moment. The observed baby's mother responded with a hug at those moments when separateness became too much. On one occasion, the baby lay on her back day-dreaming and pushing herself in a circle on the kitchen floor behind the mother. The observer moved slightly, profoundly disturbing the unintegrated baby who rushed to her mother for the hug of reassurance she needed. On another visit, the baby played with the wash-basket with the mother present. Immersed in play, the baby became angry at the contents of the basket. Her shouting crescendo continued until anger overtook her and she smacked the clothes in the basket. Upset, she ran again to the mother. At this time, when the mother is disillusioning the baby, immediate mending is important. Whether the impingement comes from outside (first example) or inside (second example), the hugs prevent trauma and the experience is then ego and boundary enhancing.

In this third section, we look at handling as the sensitive way in which the mother takes the baby through the processes of babycare. Through handling, the mother helps the baby feel more confident about the impact his actions have on the world. By handling, the mother builds on the sensitivity she has had to the baby's need for a period of hesitation or formlessness. She proves to the baby that she not only waits for the spontaneous gestures as discussed in the section on holding, but survives, welcomes, and in fact enjoys them. In the observation, for example, the mother permitted the baby's dressing to take much longer than was necessary for her to have her clothes put on but the baby was then able to experience herself going through the process and learned what her presence meant for her mother. After the steady positioning of the baby in the early months, dressing became an elaborate affair to which the mother and the baby both contributed. As she got older, the baby predicted when she needed to put her arm or leg up. The mother did not rush the baby, rather she enjoyed watching her daughter's "antics" and her increasing sense of herself. Later, after her pyjamas came off, the baby and the mother played at tickling the baby's tummy. Baby smacked her tummy and stretched out her arms as if to say "I'm here!" The constancy and evenness in the mother's introduction of the subject of dressing at the beginning, followed by an allowance for the period of hesitation and encouragement of the baby's "doings", gave her daughter the confidence to play in the stage of relative dependence. The baby was able to feel spontaneous and real.

The mother's encouragement of the baby's "doing" helps his growing sense of self in another way, too. She repeatedly shows him that in the same way as she has survived his greedy attacks of feeding, she also survives his "doing" (fantasied destruction) in the wider environment (Winnicott, 1955, 1958). Each time he asserts his existence in the world by an action, the baby sees that the mother is still herself and has in fact not been destroyed or altered. Her survival without retaliation allows him to tolerate the destructive aspect of his personality. He feels more whole and spontaneous because he sees that his deeds which, unconsciously he feared would destroy her, have in fact made her happy.

Because the mother has enjoyed the baby's company and actions by her sensitive handling of him, he can let a desire build and risk acting on it. One evening at the observation, the children played under the mother's watchful eye. Her two brothers, who were in rambunctious mood, tussled on the floor in an ownership dispute over a toy weapon but the baby and her mother remained unfazed. The baby, insulated from danger by the mother's presence, lay right beside the boys as they wrestled. Then, taking an interest in the disputed toy, she calmly crawled over the wrestlers and brought the toy to the mother so that they could investigate it together. Due also to the mother's consistent and willing response to her, the baby had an expectation that others would have the same response and speak to her. While she sat in her seat in the middle of the sitting-room floor during another visit, her excited vocalising demanded a greeting from anyone who passed by. This is how she gained acknowledgement from each of her brothers in turn as they came in to watch television. When ensconced, she shouted until they pulled her over, including her in the activity. Through her experience of the mother over time, the baby felt entitled to be welcomed and acknowledged and her sense of herself was such that she acted confidently now to make this happen even in her mother's absence.

The analytic setting as transitional phenomena in relative dependence

We can see from the example immediately above that what goes well between the baby and the mother can be reproduced when the mother is no longer present and thus used throughout the rest of life. In this and the next two sections, I revisit the concepts from the stage of relative dependence, showing, first, that the analytic space is where the patient may first encounter the transitional phenomena he needs to bridge his inside with outer reality. In the next section, I note how deficits in the three tasks of the original environmental provision manifest in the adult analytic situation. Lastly, I explore the way in which the therapist's role reflects the mother's three functions in the original setting.

Winnicott believed that "the natural thing is playing, and the highly sophisticated twentieth-century phenomenon is psychoanalysis" (1971c, p. 56). For him, psychotherapy *takes place in the overlap of two areas of playing, that of the patient and that of the therapist*" (p. 51, author's emphasis). It involves two people playing. The initial work therefore involves bringing the patient to the place where he can play. In analysis and babycare, the emphasis is on lived and shared experience felt as reliable over time. When the person has sufficient trust and boundary, this then produces an overlapping "space between", to which both members of the couple contribute. The capacity for playing depends on experience. The important thing is the creation of a space where the patient can experience held formlessness and within which he discovers something for himself. Winnicott said that only when sufficient holding has already resulted in playing does interpretation help. For the patient at the stage of relative dependence both holding and interpretation are important. The emphasis is sometimes on management and setting, as with the merged baby in the stage of absolute dependence, and at others it is on the kind of understanding and relating done by two whole and separate people.

It seems only logical then that on the analytic journey towards independence that transitional phenomena arise and there has, in fact, been extensive writing on the use of transitional objects in the analytic setting by regressed patients (Greenson, 1995; Parrish, 1995; Volkan & Kavanaugh, 1995). These preverbal symbols of reliability and care help the patient's transition from merger towards independence. For some patients, the evidence of the setting's importance is in the person of the therapist; for others it is in the physical setting. A patient can use features in the consulting room as an extension of himself and a symbol of the therapist's holding.

On her last session one such patient commented that if she ever saw the same wallpaper as is in the consulting room again she would get a jolt. On her first session, another patient said, after a break, that she was happy to get back to "her beautiful pictures".

At this time, which is at the end of merger and at the beginning of the negotiation of separateness, the part of the setting which resides in the therapist comes to light.

These objects seem important as much for the fact that they are real because they have come from outside as for the fact that they represent the analytic setting for the patient. They bridge inner and outer realities, as much conceived of as perceived, and serve to soothe the patient in times of anxiety and panic.

A certain patient used a number of "phrases" and pieces of "advice" as transitional objects. They came from outside and yet, in their significance, were also created by the patient. The words of the phrases came from the therapist (outside) and the new meanings were added by the patient (inside) by using images which came to the therapist's mind whilst the patient was speaking and which she reported to the patient as images with no prescriptive aspect.

Sometimes the curative effect is in both the physical holding of the setting and the psychical holding of the therapist's live interest.

This is the case for a patient who has a dual diagnosis of learning disability and bipolar depression. His caregiver has died and he is displaced in temporary residence with discontinuity of all his relationships. His ability to talk about himself is limited emotionally and he prefers to say he is his favourite singer or film star. His medication sometimes makes him sleepy and difficult to understand, increasing his feeling of isolation.

This person's use of concrete objects is significant and he is very sensitive to the physical detail of the setting. He comments on the fixtures in the room. Comments back from the therapist seem to strengthen a link; his reality sense is bolstered by the fact that they both see the same thing. The beginning of playing or transitional space is evidenced by the fact of time spent looking together at the same thing—living an experience together but in a very concrete way. This experience of being together allows him to integrate his sense of himself. There is one time and place that stays the same, one relationship which is reliable and can be used as a transitional object. He brings photographs from other parts of his life or disrupted relationships of the past to expand this emergent transitional space. He can use the reliability of the setting to piece himself together, to make bridges by which he can begin to feel separate and whole.

The patient's limited growth in relative dependence

In this section, we look at the limits to the patient's playing which arise from the deficits in the original environment. Although an adult patient lives independently and gets to therapy, holding is still essential at this stage. If one has not had the mother's auxiliary ego in infancy, the ensuing unheld formlessness is linked with disintegration, chaos, terror, and psychotic anxiety. In contrast to healthy failure, Failure (with a capital "F") is the trauma that cannot be borne without a break in continuity of being, chaos, and the loss to the self of all that has gone before.

One patient who has experienced Failure at the stage of relative dependence has difficulty parenting her children. Brought up in a group home herself, she finds she cannot sit with her children. She likes to sit with her partner who makes her feel safe. She is puzzled at her differing reactions. The children may join her while she does something else—when she bakes, for example. In the sessions there are long episodes of diarying her week's events without reference to the personal significance for herself. She is "baking" in the session, as she does with her children and as the staff in the group home busied themselves with their chores when she yearned for their full attention. She has a shaky time sense that comes of traumatic impingement and relies on siblings' reports for a continuum of childhood. Her "bits" extend over space and over time and she cannot play without first experiencing a reliable setting, the therapist's live interest and care over time, to strengthen her boundary and make her feel intact.

I have shown already the good effects of object presenting, when the mother presents herself as a mirror to her baby. In this way she enhances the baby's sense of self by being merged or separate according to the need which he signals to her. However, when the mother looks at the baby and her face shows only her own mood or defences, Winnicott says that the baby loses the opportunity for legitimate omnipotence and primary creativity. Perception takes what is the rightful place of apperception. The bridge of trust is damaged and what is lost is "a two-way process in which self-enrichment alternates with the discovery of meaning in the world of seen things" (Winnicott, 1967a, p. 151). Bad experience often feels like a lack of a bridge for the person between his inner life and outer reality. One's capacity to feel real and confident in one's interactions with the world is compromised if the mother presents herself in this way.

A patient's mother presented herself sporadically and unreliably and never wanted to spend time with her. The patient refers to herself as a "bouncing ball". Her mother constantly dropped her, promising to be back soon (days or weeks). Feeling herself a burden, the patient stayed quiet so as to keep safe these varied, begrudging and temporary resting places. She was always at some point in the trajectory of her "bouncing-ball" self-image; catapulted, in unsupported motion, or falling. Once when the mother stormed out, the patient ran calling after her but she "never even looked back", and the patient returned for another indefinite stay.

At six years old, this patient regularly sat on the step of her mother's house after school awaiting her return, only to give up hours later and resort to a relative's house. Her mother's presentation of herself was not of the constancy that allowed the patient to negotiate risk and novelty with a sense of safety and confidence. In fact, her unreliable presentation of herself was in the nature of a surprise demand rather than an expectable adaptation. This patient did not have the "present absence", "absent presence" or "stillness" in which the child's transitional space builds. Her mother definitely was not still there, having been temporarily forgotten. The patient finds it hard to let a desire build. Her "period of hesitation" is followed only by the most timid of gestures. She once tapped on the door so lightly for her appointment, that no one heard, recreating the "no one home" scenario that she experienced with mother in childhood. It is hard to ask for things for herself. It is safer to be "inaudible" and "invisible", and this is reflected in her tentative and cautious use of the session where she is at once fearful but hopeful of finding a reliable mirror to help her replace compliance with spontaneity.

In the developmental section, I showed the importance of the mother's sensitive handling of the baby. I showed how her non-retaliatory welcoming of the baby's "doing" helps the baby to integrate the loving and instinctual aspects of his personality, making him feel real and in harmony with his world. Often the limits set on the maturational processes by the non-survival or retaliation of the parent in the original setting is paralleled in the adult's curtailed use of the analysis.

For one such patient, feeling a lack of integration and an inability to use the therapy is linked to her memory, when a toddler, of being frantically dragged by the arm about the city by her mother whilst being repeatedly told she was too slow. So painful was it that she remembers her childhood impulse, on walking past a body of water, to throw herself in. Another such patient had, throughout his childhood, a neglectful home situation. During occasional angry cleaning frenzies, his father had a habit of putting the children's possessions in the bin. This was felt to be a putting aside of the evidence of the children's "being" and "doing". Once, when things were really bad, the patient took out his favourite possession, his toy soldiers, and buried them in the garden but continued to take secret pleasure in knowing their location. The therapist's attempts at maintaining the frequency of sessions were refused by the patient. Reduced frequency had become a matter of pride and associated with increased independence. Now, with a frequency of once per month, the patient telephones at the midpoint to check the session details. It is obvious that there is much invested in the physical aspects of this setting.

The sessions work in the same way as the secret knowledge of the location of the soldiers. The soldiers and sessions are valued more for their contribution to an isolated area of fantasying than for their symbolic bridging of the patient's inside and outside. In the patient's thinking, they contribute to the sense of agency and omnipotent control rather than to real playing on the border of the inner and outer realities. This shows that the "personalisation" process, that is, the integration of psyche and soma (Winnicott, 1962c), is interrupted, replacing mothering with a split-off caretaker "mind-psyche" so that the patient lives in his head and does not properly inhabit his body. It also reveals the limits of the patient's "realisation" in time and space. The telephone calls keep the interval between sessions in $x + y$ and prevent it from running into traumatic z time. Actually playing with the soldiers or coming to sessions, however, would involve the patient bodily as well as imaginatively. It would take up time and space in the same way that scattered soldiers, the dangerously messy evidence of his physical presence in the world, drew his father's anger. For such a person much work will be needed providing a non-retaliatory and surviving setting before playing can predominate in the session between two whole and separate people.

The analyst's function in relative dependence

At the stage of relative dependence, the therapist must complete the three parts of the mother function, taking account now of the ever-changing levels of separateness/unity which the patient needs. In this section, I deal again with the three mother functions, starting with holding. The therapist's auxiliary ego holds the fragmented patient in the safe and limited formlessness of the session, helping him to become ultimately more real. In order to feel real, the above mentioned patient who was brought up in a group home seemed to need the therapist to know, live through, and hold together her pieces of experience, her "bits". Just as she felt safer sitting with her partner, she wanted the therapist to sit with her through the whole week. Through her interested attention the therapist integrates the bits of the patient. Winnicott says:

> An example of unintegration phenomena is provided by the very common experience of the patient who proceeds to give every detail of the week-end and feels contented at the end [...] to be known in all his bits and pieces [...] means to feel integrated at least in the person of the analyst [...] an infant who has had no one person to gather his bits together starts with a handicap in his own self-integrating task [...] or at any rate cannot maintain integration with confidence. (Winnicott, 1945, p. 150)

Something else is also happening. The therapist allows the patient, for the first time, to have the "period of hesitation" that is the prerequisite of the truly spontaneous gesture. She waits as the patient takes her own time, sets the pace, and lives the time in a way which was not possible when as a child she was dealt with as one of a group. The patient gives convoluted preambles to a basic point. It is easy for the therapist to think that the patient is wasting time, avoiding issues or resisting, yet the patient considers the therapy to be vital. This "period of hesitation" of the spatula observation technique when applied to the analytic space, is Winnicott's (1941) reformulation of the concept of resistance. It is the therapist's rationale for waiting and witnessing the patient's apparently meaningless associations, what Winnicott calls the "nonsense", which is the necessary prelude to the "overlapping play area". The challenge to the therapist and the patient here is to risk waiting, to hold the formlessness and apparent nonsense until some real meaning emerges which gives form and cohesion. The therapist must trust that her live presence and the patient's unintegration over time will create the space in which the patient can risk a gesture.

Part of the holding function of the therapist is to fail the patient in order to help him feel real. Patients are very sensitive to small changes in the setting at this stage. For this reason, the therapist may, for example, defer starting with a new patient until after a holiday break. The patient would not be ready for any failure because trust would not have been built up over time, or sufficient reliability introjected, to take the patient through the separation. At the same time however, a failure on the therapist's part (for example, arriving late) can make more real the separateness of the patient and therapist.

The therapist's object-presenting function at this stage involves the paradoxical tasks of maintaining both the boundary and the space between herself and the patient at the same time. As has been stated, this requires constant attention as the amounts of separateness and unity which the patient can manage is in perpetual flux. For the person who has not been responsively presented with boundaries at this stage, "unit status" is not confidently established. The therapist must present herself in a way which accounts for the two kinds of difficulty which arise here—the patient may feel too much or too little separateness between himself and the therapist. This sometimes manifests in the search for and testing of the boundary.

A certain patient punctured and stretched the physical and time boundaries of the therapy up to the particular session in which the therapist assured her of their separateness. Her mother had been unable to present herself sensitively to her during the stage of relative dependence. In therapy, this patient needed to test the reliability and stability of the physical boundaries of the setting, as well as that part of the setting which exists in the therapist. Shortly after beginning to attend, she started to arrive early and stayed still on the couch for some time after the therapist ended the session. This reduced gradually. She spent some months going to the bathroom during, before, and/or after a session. It seemed that she was leaving there those things which she feared could not be held or which might alter her or the therapist, or both. She became upset or expressed her feelings only close to the end of each session. Then it was safe to relate a small part of her distress because the safety of separateness loomed. One day, the patient sat up off the couch in a session and said she intended to finish early. The therapist pointed out that it was she, in fact, who finished the sessions and requested that the patient continue to the end. This had the effect of making the patient better able to use the sessions. She had wanted to leave because she was upset and cried when asked to stay.

By showing the different nature of their respective roles, the therapist underlined the patient's boundary. Her feelings of upset began to be felt in the sessions and her testing of the limits of the session decreased. It seems that the patient's attempt to challenge or ignore a part of the therapist's role in ending the session had come out of a merging or erasing of the boundary between them in the patient's thinking. This thinking made it unsafe to use the time in order to relate her inner distress. In the fantasy of merger it would destroy both of them. Her ability to use the space further improved with her understanding of the therapist's separateness. Now she attends on time but not early and rises quite promptly when the session is over. It seems apposite here to note Winnicott's understanding of separation anxiety as the fear of not being able to separate without damage to the self or the mother.

The patient's vacillation at this stage between the illusion of unity and separateness makes the therapist's sensitive handling vital. At this time, when the patient risks asserting himself, proof of the survival and non-retaliatory response of the therapist will be needed, as well as a welcoming of the patient's spontaneous doing. The therapist has to achieve the balance which allows the patient to be spontaneous, experience his own effort, and feel real without feeling dropped or disillusioned prematurely. The therapist must maintain a consistent manner, for example in relation to the case of the patient already mentioned whose angry father put his possessions in the bin. Any change in the therapist's manner may be taken as her retaliation or destruction as a result of the patient's "doing"—in this case, his interference with the arrangements about the room or his failure to take up the more frequent sessions. In the same way, changed times, cancelled appointments, or alterations to the room may in other cases be taken in fantasy as the therapist's non-survival or retaliation. In the above example of the patient who cannot bring herself to tap loudly enough on the door, the therapist must note the barely audible signal of her arrival and attend to the meaning of the communication. The patient seems to be saying "Listen carefully, your interested attention is important to me, but I do not expect it and so I only dare ask in a timid whisper". The therapist must continue here to leave the space for this small gesture and welcome it when it arrives whilst constantly holding the patient.

The therapist may need to do much work, countering the patient's first experience, in order to bring him to the point where he can make a restitutive gesture. This is the case with the patient with dual diagnosis mentioned in the first section on transitional phenomena. His caregiver has died and he blames himself, causing his spontaneity to be inhibited. The therapist's reliability is proof of her survival. She welcomes his "real" self and his "doings" so that he believes he can make restitution for his fantasied destruction by, for example, offering to fix things in the room. He plays a little, since his confidence in the reliability of this small space has grown. Sometimes he just comes in, sits, hums, dozes, or drinks the coke he has in his pocket. In these sessions, he seems to relax more, to be spontaneous and to recapture a happier time when he was company for a mother-figure and they watched television together.

Summary

Looking first at the nature of transitional phenomena and playing, I showed that relative dependence is the stage of transitional space. I then looked at the baby's growth and the mother's changing functions, using examples from a baby observation. Next, I turned my attention to the analytic space where I explored the transitional phenomena as they arise in therapy. I looked first at the patient's growth and then at the changes to the analyst's function at this stage, using case examples for illustration.

CHAPTER FOUR

Towards independence—the whole person

In this chapter, I look at the concepts attaching to the third stage: when the person goes towards independence. I look first at the expansion and further internalisation of transitional space in the developmental situation, noting the changes in the baby and in the mother's role at this time, and I also refer to the lifelong nature of the expansion. Next, I show how Winnicott's consideration of the mother function is useful clinically in two ways. First, it helps us deal with those patients for whom the difficulty is of a preoedipal nature. Second, it allows our practice to be more flexible and to account for the complexity of human experience, by recognising the dialectical nature of the transference and real relationships.

The baby's movement towards independence

As we have seen, in absolute and relative dependence, the capacity to be alone first develops in the presence of the mother when the holding experienced by the baby has been good enough. Then, "through the accumulation of memories of care, the projection of personal needs and the introjection of care details [the baby develops] confidence in the environment" (Winnicott, 1960a, p. 46). Trust, memories, and greater intellectual understanding allow the baby to internalise the transitional space. Here, the baby has the capacity to live without actual care and expand the transitional space to other areas of his life. He has in himself the capacity to keep inside and outside separate yet interrelated and to balance their contributions in his experience. An interchange is set up between inner and outer realities which results in one being enriched by the other.

At nine months, the baby I observed was able to hold her initial impulse to cry when her mother went out to the clothesline. She watched her mother through the patio doors, tapping them and saying "ma-ma" repeatedly. Here she used that part of the transitional space they shared and which she had internalised to contain her anxiety. In the good enough situation at this stage, there is a robust boundary between inside and outside, a shared area of experience, and a confidence in an ever-growing environment, so that life is an enjoyable adventure. I noticed this appetite for novelty in the observation baby who felt restricted towards the end of the visits. She often looked for her coat which in turn signaled going out. On one occasion she was wearing it in play as the visit began, and on another she stood under the hallstand, crying until the mother gave it to her. This is the space of whole separate people who are still connected, however, by a vast area of shared understanding. On the last visit, the baby knew immediately to come to the table when the mother made tea; although she now had a sense of herself as a separate person, this was an example of the shared area of understanding connecting herself and her mother. In this last stage of the transitional process, the boundary between inside and outside can expand into all areas of the growing child's life. This is the oedipal situation.

The mother's changing role

In the good situation, the mother builds redundancy into her initial role and knows that her continuous presence is no longer necessary or desirable. She also acknowledges the difference between her needs and those of the baby. The observation mother was aware of her reluctance to let go and that contrary to her experience with the other children, she had felt no hurry to get the baby her first shoes. She laughed at herself for leaving the Mother's Day cards and flowers on the mantelpiece so long after the event. She was angry but gracious in her upset at the ending of the observation, as it marked the end of her daughter's babyhood. She balanced this by the welcome and pride she showed in her daughter's precocity. Although the mother's role changes at this stage and she and her child become two separate people, they continue to be connected through all their shared experiences. On the last visit, the mother had given the baby a packet of candy sticks and now asked her to share, saying to the observer, "Do you remember that these were called toy cigarettes?" It was as though the mother was reassuring herself in regard to her baby that the more things change, the more they stay the same. The baby observation and babyhood were over but those experiences which she and her baby had shared together would enrich those to come.

The lifelong expansion of the transitional space

Winnicott felt that in health we never become completely independent. We depend on the other for our independence, self-knowledge, and capacity to feel real and live creatively. The baby neither becomes completely independent of the mother nor vice versa. "'Towards independence' describes the strivings of the toddler child and of the child at puberty" (Winnicott, 1963b, p. 92). The process that took place between the mother and the baby happens again between the adolescent and the wider society as "the child is identified with society, because local society is a sample of the self's personal world as well as being a sample of truly external phenomena" (Winnicott, 1963b, p. 91). On the strength of the prototype in the first dyad, the individual now extends and enriches his transitional space to find himself through professional, social, aesthetic, cultural, and spiritual experiences as he first did through his mother. Adults also must continue with "the process of growing and of growing up, since they do but seldom reach to full maturity" (p. 92). Winnicott felt that adult life starts when, in society—through work and perhaps marriage—one finds a place between copying and defying one's parents. Then "the individuals one by one climb out of [this] area [...] of dependence towards independence" (p. 92).

The analytic situation

Through psychoanalytic thinking, Winnicott made explicit and conscious Freud's unconscious deference to the importance of the mother function in the analytic space, so that its curative property might be harnessed. With his three stage model of dependence, he shows how transitional space is internalised in the first couple and in the analytic couple. His contribution offers a flexible starting point which is adaptive to the individual's need and which could be viewed as preceeding and extending the classical method.

When the original transitional space has not been internalised and extended by the patient, Winnicott advises that the focus in the analytic situation is on the therapeutic alliance, based on the reality principle and the dyadic relationship between the "real" analyst and the "real" person of the patient. Winnicott has been called "the father" of the therapeutic alliance (Grotstein, 1990), which stresses the constant variables of ego-relatedness, the environment mother, separateness, and difference. It deals with the slow-moving bounded energy associated with the conscious, ego function, secondary process, and the fixity and stability that go with that. On the contrary, Freud emphasises the transference relationship, which is inextricably linked to resistance and the oedipal situation of the three-bodied relationship. He deals with the "transferent" analyst of "primative imagoes" and with the fast changing dynamics of the unbounded, mobile energy of the unconscious, the inner life, fantasy, primary processes and the id. From Winnicott's point of view, Freud emphasises id-relatedness, the object mother, unity, and sameness.

The usefulness of Winnicott's approach is assessed by Margaret Little who, after her first two analyses based on classical interpretation, still felt a persistent wish "to be somebody" and suffered fears she felt "only children feel". At the time, the classical interpretations, relating to oedipal conflict, were of a developmental stage that was beyond Little. Her difficulties were of a dyadic nature and the issue of what was or was not real needed clarification from the therapist taking account of the patient's delicate sense of reality. Following her (successful) third analysis with Winnicott, she explains:

> The experience of being "mothered" is truly mutative in that it resolves the anxiety concerning survival and identity by providing reassurance and continuity of being. Awareness of being real, recognition of what is inner or outer, ability to fantasise and to distinguish fantasy from reality, to symbolise, to relate to others in a way that was previously impossible and to mature, first to the "depressive position" (Klein, 1935) or "stage of concern" (Winnicott, 1950)

and later to the oedipal level, follow as in normal development, helped on by whatever maturity had been achieved before. (Little, 1990, p. 90)

With sufficient experience of the reliability of the analytic setting over time, Little went on to work through her difficulties that were of a pre-dyadic and dyadic nature, and continued through with a classical analysis of a triangular nature. Winnicott said: "It is not that Freud is wrong about the father and the libidinal tie that becomes repressed. But it has to be noted that a proportion of persons in the world do not reach to the Oedipus complex" (1969, p. 241). Like Little, these people will benefit from the experience of the reliable holding of the setting before being able to benefit from the classical approach.

In the interest of balance, Winnicott emphasised both therapeutic alliance and transference. For him the constant and dynamic variables are of equal importance and rely on each other for their significance. He saw the interdependence of setting and process, dyad and triad, object mother and environment mother. In terms of maturational equivalents he saw the reliance of "doing" on "being", spontaneous gesture on "period of hesitation", of dependence on independence, of inside on outside, self on other. The real and transferential relationship of the patient with the analyst may be seen as two strands in a dialectical thread spanning the duration of the analysis. Both variable types seem always to be involved, but in varying degrees, so that what is in the background in one session takes the foreground in another. For Freud, the archeological dig results in an authoritarian handing down to the patient of an uncovered definitive truth by the analyst. For Winnicott, the setting must be first secure, then the couple find/create meaning together in an overlapping play area.

This concept of overlapping play area, or third area of experience, introduced by Winnicott, suggests that he thought in terms of triangles other than the oedipal one. Indeed, he gained recognition for the therapeutic alliance only to achieve balance with the transference and to make it possible to emphasise the area between the two. Winnicott (1963c) wrote of a dream he had in which he sees his three "selves". There is "I" the destroyed, "I" the destroyer, and the "I" that in the dream has woken up and knows he has dreamed the other two. He says that without this third "I" the other two must remain split. In analysis, the split is between the constant and dynamic variables of the dialectic couples: outer and inner, reality and fantasy, separation and unity, conscious and unconscious. It is also between the real and transferential therapist. The split is resolved as the third part of the observing therapist knows how much he understands the patient on the one hand (therapeutic alliance) or empathises on the other (transference). The third part of the adult patient facilitates his awareness of the discrepancy between his responses that are a result of transference and those which are his adult responses to the real therapist. This "third area" of experience makes possible the flexible and adaptive response which comes from the whole person recognising the relative contributions of each variable at any one time.

This can be seen in the following example.

A patient has an ambivalent relationship with her mother. As a child she witnessed the acute disharmony between the mother and the father and her allegiances swung from the mother to the father and back again to the mother in adolescence. The patient was a favourite with the father and had a good relationship with him in every way, other than on the issue of his marriage, whereas the mother was an unhappy and demanding figure, portraying herself always as a helpless victim whilst attempting to control her family. The patient's concern about the mother's wellbeing was mixed with the anger at her constant interference and criticism. The patient saw the mother's final pregnancy late in life as removing her mother's chance of happiness and vowed to her mother that she would take over the mothering of this baby. Her motivation in doing this can be seen to come at once from unresolved difficulties of both a dyadic and oedipal nature. When the patient became pregnant she could not go home because of the mother's interference. Now back living with her children near her widowed mother, the patient's contact with her mother is fraught. She cannot tolerate the contact for which she yearns.

When the therapist telephoned to inquire about the patient after she has missed a session, it was received differently on different occasions. On one occasion, it was a welcome and heartfelt act of concern. On another it was an intrusion, a policing of the therapy in a forceful and unwelcome way. It seems that on both occasions the transference was a maternal one. The patient's welcoming response was to the yearned-for mother of the dyadic relationship. Her unwelcoming response was to the mother of the triangular relationship who leaned on the patient emotionally when they were rivals, was an intrusive figure during pregnancy, did not allow her to break free of the childish relationship, and who contributed to the loss of the father for whose affection she competed.

Winnicott's model of the analytic situation accounts for all aspects of this complicated mother–daughter relationship. It provides for the dyadic and three-person aspects. It accounts for the therapeutic relationship and the transference. It acknowledges the interaction of the real and fantasy aspects in the patient's whole experience. In differing degrees on different occasions, the patient knows when her reaction is more than she can account for by the real situation. Holding what she knows of the real therapist against what she feels in the transference is possible by virtue of this third reflective part of the experiencing whole person. For Winnicott, two live people, the patient and the therapist, are contributing into the overlapping space of their shared experience. At the same time, through the therapist's holding, transitional space builds up inside the patient, making an experiencing area where the patient can accommodate both the transference and the working relationship. What is important for Winnicott, therefore, is the analyst's whole response to the whole patient. He is more for a reliable and predictable response from the whole person of the therapist who is attuned and spontaneous than for a neutral screen, which presumes that the therapist can in some way detach herself from the situation. Winnicott's approach also allows for flexibility and playing in the therapist's understanding of the patient while accounting for the complexity of the patient's experience.

In understanding that the dynamics and constants of the analytic situation inform each other, define each other, and negate each other, Winnicott understood that there will never be a time when ego replaces id, because one exists by virtue of the other. Rather, there is a move towards integration that is never complete and the dialectical tension continues in the enjoyable and fulfilled life of the person who lives in the third area of transitional space.

Summary

In this chapter, I looked at how life proceeds in adulthood, with the internalisation and expansion of transitional space, for the baby who has had a good start. I looked at the way in which Winnicott's thinking may be seen to complement Freud's work by extending its reach backwards to the infant's very early development. The dyadic themes stressed by Winnicott may be considered alongside the three-person oedipal concerns to make for a flexible responsiveness on the part of the whole therapist towards the whole patient, reflecting the complex nature of human experience.

Complete independence is neither fully achieved nor healthy. Rather, each person lives in dialectical tension in the third place of experience that is between inside and outside, unity and separateness, dependence and independence, fantasy and reality, conception and perception, and contributed to by both.

In a successful situation, the separateness/unity paradox spans from the first relationship up to the potential space that connects and separates the individual from a rich and meaningful life in all its spheres.

CHAPTER FIVE

A baby observation

As well as being of interest in itself, it is hoped that the following observation brings to life the instances cited in the previous chapters. The observation is written in the form of notes made after almost every visit with some notes more extensive than others. It is written in the language used in the course of those visits rather than anything more formal and makes obvious the imperfections in my execution of my role as an observer. After this chapter there is a further chapter with a summary report on the baby observation, of the kind that might be written as part of a professional training. It is hoped that it will serve to illuminate and consolidate what has gone before.

Introductory visit

Date: 8 pm on 20 November

Eilis (pronounced "Ailish") and I first spoke on the telephone when I called her when she was approximately six months pregnant. I introduced myself and outlined what would be involved in the baby observation. She explained her reasons for being interested in being involved.

We exchanged contact details and I suggested that she take time to think about it and to discuss it with her partner and family. About two weeks later she called back to say that she wished to proceed and I made an arrangement to meet herself and her partner, Mac.

I telephoned before I went over, for directions, and Eilis answered. She explained where she lived, and also that Mac would have to go out soon after I had called. When I got there, Eilis answered the door and brought me in to the sitting-room. She switched off the TV and explained that Mac was upstairs getting the children settled in bed. Eilis talked to me about the size of her "bump" and then Mac came down stairs. Mac asked me first about where I lived and my own family and then about the observation arrangements. He asked me about my work and this lead to them briefly discussing a relative with a learning diffi- culty. Mac asked me if I knew a psychologist whom he had come across and who had done work on animal behaviour. I did not. He told me that he had done a science degree in the university which I had also attended and I told him that the people on his course had always been good at volunteering as subjects in the years when I had been doing my experimental psychology course.

Mac went to check on the boys (aged eight, six, and four) because of noise coming from upstairs and then Eilis and I talked about how the children were getting very excited about Santa. Her oldest boy had been upset before he went to bed because he couldn't decide what to ask for whereas the middle boy, she said, could not care less. Eilis talked about the adjustment the boys would have to make for the new baby— especially the four year-old, Gavan. She said that she was looking for- ward to having only one baby to look after this time as the others were all babies together.

When Mac came back I asked him if he would mind my visits to see the baby when he was not there. He said that he did not and won- dered what they might get out of the exercise. I said that it was really a case of them doing something for me and that when the observation was over, I could give a summary of milestones but that that was all. They then talked about their efforts at recording the others when they were born. They were delighted to have the video of the last baby being born.

I asked them how they had met as Eilis's family were not living in this country and they told me that it all began when Mac's friend got a job abroad and Mac had gone over for a party. They had had a long distance relationship for the three years while Eilis was still in university and Eilis remarked that her mother used to wonder why she brought all her "style" with her on "study weekend" visits she used make to her college friend's hometown (where she would be meeting Mac).

Mac had to go out at this point and I said that I would go too. He went first though and he said that he would ring me when the baby was born and I could go in and see the baby in the hospital if I'd like. I said that they could wait to see how they were feeling and that I would love to go in if that was alright.

When Mac was gone Eilis talked a little more about how things would be when the baby arrived and about how she was more tired this time than in previous pregnancies. I said that I thought that she had a neat "bump" and she said that she felt enormous and that she couldn't wait to get her body back and go jogging again.

I wished her a Happy Christmas and said I'd see her sometime in the New Year around the expected delivery date and that it may be a little later than that because hadn't she said that the other children had arrived late. She agreed that they had been and we said our good-byes then.

Visit one

Date: 2 pm on 18 January

Age of baby: 1 day

On returning home on the evening of the 17 January, I got a call on my answering machine from Eilis from the maternity hospital saying that her baby girl, Aisling (meaning "dream", and pronounced "Ashling") Lucy, had been born at a quarter to four that morning, weighing eight pounds.

The next day, I went to the hospital to see the baby. Eilis was in bed with her baby lying beside her. The baby was plump-faced, little, with lots of red-brown hair and some red blotches on her forehead. She did not open her eyes at any stage during the visit. Eilis lifted the baby up and held her for a moment and then offered the baby to me to hold. She was quite still while I held her and as I held her baby, Eilis told me about the labour and delivery. The baby became heavier and soundly asleep in my arms and I asked Eilis would I put her in her crib and she said she would take her.

After a while the baby started to fidget and move her legs and arms up and down. Eilis put her on her shoulder and after a short protest she seemed to be enjoying this position and relaxed. Mother continued to talk quietly and suddenly the baby seemed to be gripped by a pain and tucked her knees up in front of her. Eilis spoke to her and she calmed a little and started to nod about at her mother's shoulder for food. She then put her head on Eilis's shoulder and became quiet for a while.

The next time that the baby moved, she screamed loudly. She flailed out her hands and they began to shake. Eilis held her up straight on her knee with her hand under her chin and rubbed her back. She continued to wriggle and this did not help her sufficiently. Then Eilis tried to feed her, speaking to her as she did. There continued a long process of Eilis trying to latch the baby on to her breast. The baby would suck loudly and then let go but continue to suck. The baby did not seem to distinguish between the breast and her own mouth but screamed angrily at not being comforted. Eilis found this tolerably anxiety-provoking. She said that this baby was drowsier than the others had been and was less well able to feed and that this process of having difficulty getting her to feed had been going on earlier that day. Eventually the baby stayed feeding for a little longer and when she let go this time screamed even more angrily. Eilis decided to try the left breast and had a significantly greater success so that the baby latched on almost immediately and fed for several minutes before falling soundly asleep as I was leaving.

Visit two

9 am on 26 January

8 days

This was my second time to see Aisling and my first to see her at home. Eilis answered the door to me and brought me into the sitting room where Aisling was sitting propped up in the corner of the couch. She was wearing a babygro and cardigan and was wrapped in a blanket with her hands out in front of her. She was sleeping but her face had filled out and though her eyes were closed they were less tightly closed so that her lashes were visible now and they also were dark. The marks on her face had faded and the one on her hairline had faded too. Eilis said that she was beautiful and said somewhat regretfully that she had gotten big already. She said that she was happy that the marks on her forehead had faded and was happy that they were not going to be noticeable. Aisling pouted and moved a little when Eilis spoke. The telephone rang and Eilis went to answer it. The baby became still and five minutes went by without her moving at all apart from breathing. In the twenty minutes that Eilis was out of the room Aisling fanned and relaxed her hands three times and hiccupped twice.

When Eilis came back she said she would do as she normally would and looked at me to check that this was okay. She lifted Aisling and put her into her "Moses basket" and covered her with two blankets. Aisling moved about and made faces for a few seconds and then seemed to go asleep again. She then turned her head to the left and stayed that way. Aisling changed her breathing and went pink and then red. She moved her head to the centre and started to make faces and puckered her lips. Her eyes started to flicker and Eilis said, "She's dreaming." She said that she did not want to take the baby out in the frost but that the boys wanted to show her off at school. She said that she needed to wash out her pram and said that Mac discovered when he went to assemble her new buggy that there was a piece missing.

Eilis gave me a cup of coffee and sat down with one herself. She said that she did not want to become too absorbed in the baby to the exclusion of the other children, or so that they would feel left out. She said, "It's difficult when they always want to hold the baby." She said that she had seen her friend become very absorbed in her baby to the exclusion of the older children and that this might be related to the fact that one of the children was now not liked by adults and was a pain in the neck.

When I said it was time to go and asked could I make another time Eilis seemed surprised that the hour was up. When I gave her the time she said she would write that down as she was a bit "doolally" but not as much as when she was expecting her first child. I followed Eilis into the kitchen to return my coffee cup and give her the date. I took a last look at Aisling as I went through the hall and she looked like she was waking up and might be looking for food soon.

Visit three

9 am on 5 February

19 days

Today Pol, the eldest child, opened the door to me. The children were off school on mid-term break. When I went into the sitting room Eilis was feeding baby Aisling on the sofa. I sat down and Eilis turned Aisling around for my benefit, so that I could look at her face. She had grown and filled out and her eyes were wide open and looking around. Aisling's hair has grown and it gives her an older look. When Eilis started to talk to me and say that "they are all mad about the baby", Aisling was quiet and gazed up at her face with a look of concentration.

The three boys were in the room for a few minutes. The two younger boys, Donal and Gavan, were playing cards in their pyjamas and the TV was on. The eldest, Pol, was reading a book on the other sofa. Eilis put Aisling to her breast and she latched on immediately and fed easily. I asked if she was feeding alright now and Eilis looked at the baby lovingly and said, "She's as good as gold, she's a perfect baby, never a moment of bother." She added that the baby fed and slept well. The baby pulled back from the breast and Eilis said, "She's very clever now. She knows to do that when she's had enough or when the milk is coming too fast." Then Aisling got sick and there was a collective "yeuch" from the boys and Pol went out of the room. Eilis asked Donal to get a tissue and he said Pol's gone and Eilis said, "I don't think he is." Donal went and got one. Eilis cleaned her baby up and put her on the pouffe in front of her and changed her nappy. I went around the other side to look at Aisling's face as she turned her face away towards the window once she was put flat. She took the process calmly and shivered twice and her eyes widened when she was having her navel wiped.

Gavan, the four year old asked for a chocolate bar and Eilis said, "no," and to "go and get dressed." The two remaining boys went upstairs for a while and then went into the kitchen and the three were having cereal and were playing together. Eilis put Aisling lying on her side on the sofa as she was washing her hands. Aisling had a look of concentration whilst looking at the pattern of the sofa and then seemed to look to the point where the arm of the chair stopped and the light of the room started. She moved her hands and arms gently. When Eilis came back and started to look at her and talk to me she stilled and found her mother's face even before Eilis touched her. Eilis put Aisling on her lap facing her and Aisling seemed to be smiling at her and mouthing silent "oohs". Eilis started to talk to me again and told me that she thinks that Aisling may have curly hair as its very strong hair and she may be a redhead. Aisling started to squirm and when she turned her head to one side Eilis took that as a sign that she was still hungry. "You're still hungry you poor pet, there, that's right," and she spoke to her until she had settled into feeding.

Aisling makes little humming noises when she is feeding. At one stage she let go and Eilis said "She knows she's doing that" as Aisling continued to smack her lips together. Eilis said that Aisling now just licks the other breast when it leaks as it does often and saves herself the bother of sucking. Aisling continued to feed for another few moments, very seriously and she then pulled her head away. Eilis said to her "I know [...] it's very hard work" as she put Aisling straight on her knee facing me and Aisling panted for a few moments. When Eilis put her back to feed again, Aisling started to "mess" and Eilis said, "She does this when she has wind or is about to do her poos." Gavan came into the room with a bowl of rice crispies and stood very close to his mother. Aisling began to squirm gently and began to pull up the right leg which was on top and straighten it again. This movement was exaggerated until Aisling pulled away altogether and started and yelled contorting her face.

Eilis sat Aisling up straight and said, "I don't rub her back if she has wind she just seems to get it up," but when Aisling screamed again she rubbed it briefly and a moment after she stopped and Aisling got sick more than the first time. Again Gavan ran and Eilis got a tissue from the side of the sofa and cleaned it up. Then Aisling went limp and relaxed and seemed to be smiling. Eilis said, "It's funny but they all really are a good help and Pol changed her dirty nappy and made a good job of it [...] but they all run a mile from her if she pukes—they are disgusted." Gavan came back in and said that he wanted to hold Aisling. Eilis arranged him, holding Aisling opposite her on the pouffe, fixing his hands. He watched Eilis with an intense and serious face while she spoke to Aisling and took this opportunity to make eye contact. He went to give her back and changed his mind a few times. Eilis said, "This boy is very gentle with his sister." I said, "She is a lucky girl to have you." He almost smiled. Eilis said, "We had the baby down at the school on Wednesday." Eilis put Aisling on the other side and she fed seriously making her humming noise. After some time the other leg, which was now on top, started to move. Eilis started to tell me about her trip with the baby over to her workplace. She said a friend drove her as she didn't want to drive that far. She added, "Although I can't see myself going back, I don't know what'll happen," and I said, "That's right, because it's a long journey isn't it?" "One hour but it's hard too, to get morning-only work. The children don't even know that I'm gone and because Mac works locally, he can take them to school." Eilis said, "You're probably dying for a cup of coffee." I said, "Not at all, I had coffee at home this morning." She said she was having one anyway and I said it was actually time for me to go. I said, "Will I come back this time next week?" and she said that it suits her if it's okay for me. Eilis walked me out, still holding Aisling at her breast.

Visit four

9 am on 12 February

26 days

When Eilis answered the door, she said, "Hello, come in, she's in there. I put her on the floor so you could see her." Aisling was in her crib lying on her tummy with her hands up on either side of her head. Eilis said that she had been putting Aisling on her tummy for the last few days as she had eaten something that upset Aisling's tummy—perhaps broccoli. She said that she had all the other children on their tummies and she thought that Aisling got relief from it. I said "She has grown" and as Eilis started to talk about her, Aisling's eyes opened slightly and started to flutter for as long as Eilis was speaking. Eilis then went into the kitchen as at one stage there was a clanging noise and Aisling jumped.

For many minutes, Aisling slept like that, motionless except for her breathing which was changing as though she were going into an even deeper sleep. Then she startled twice as though having the sensation of falling off a cliff's edge. Aisling's right hand moved a lot and then her left hand moved and she had her face turned to the right for most of the time.

Eilis came in after about twenty minutes and asked if I would like a coffee and again Aisling's eyes widened a little and fluttered. I pointed to her saying, "She has not moved all the time you were out," and Eilis said, "Oh, I know, although I think that she is getting used to the sound of my voice," and then, also about Aisling's reaction to her, "She's probably thinking it is just as well as I'd be twitching all the time as that one never shuts up!"

When Eilis went out this time, Aisling seemed to be dreaming for a while with her facial expressions changing from second to second. At one stage she put her hand towards her mouth and opened her mouth as though dreaming of the breast. At another point she seemed to smile in her sleep. She did not settle and gradually started to move her legs under her blankets. At one stage she went pink for a moment as though defecating but continued to wriggle. Aisling made low grunting noises for about tem minutes before she eventually let out two cries and Eilis came into the room and lifted her. This seemed to give instant comfort and Aisling sat on Eilis's knee with a serious expression and really looked at me. She held her head up herself and stayed still for a few seconds as though taking in my face. Her eyes are wider, and looking from one thing the other now.

Eilis sat down and put Aisling on her shoulder where she started to bob her head about as though looking for food. Eilis rubbed Aisling's back and said, "She has a pain, I can feel it." She then said, "I know what you want," and started to feed her. Aisling latched on immediately and started to gulp and Eilis said "Oh don't do that or you'll pay for it later." Aisling fed for a few minutes and then she let go and Eilis sat her up facing me. She was grimacing with wind. Ellen said, "I hope that she isn't going to be a colicky baby like Pol, he was always guzzling and would cry then for more." She told the story of Pol and then said "But it's all good news about you, isn't it?" to the baby. I asked how Aisling's name was spelled and Eilis told me. She said that she had wanted to call one of the boys after her father but thought that he'd get laughed at as it was an old-fashioned name. Eilis played with the baby's hair and said that when she is feeding Aisling she looks at her hair and that she is so different to the others and wonders with the red flecks if she could she be going to a redhead. Aisling pulled away from the breast and Eilis sat her up and said, "I can feel her tummy is all hard." She said that her babies had liked to be rubbed quite hard and then, "At least this lady does." Eilis spoke of the boys' disgust at Aisling's sick, at how messy breast-feeding is and about Aisling's nappy rash. She then asked if I would like coffee and I said that it was time for me to go and that I would let myself out and Eilis said, "Yes, would you?" We made arrangements for the next visit and I left.

Visit five

10 am on 19 February

33 days

Eilis answered the door and said, "She's in here," walking back into the sitting room. Eilis was wearing make-up and when I got into the room

Aisling was sitting in her carry chair in the middle of the room. She was sitting with her head to one side looking around her. She looked bigger and her face looked longer. Her eyes focused and she looked around the room. She looked at Eilis as she explained to me that they would be leaving at the same time as me today as they were bringing Mac's mother to see her sister who lives in a nursing home. Eilis went to get ready and I sat on the floor between Aisling and the window. Aisling had her fists tucked up at her sides. She spent a long time looking at the tiles on the fireplace which are definite shades and patterned. She then got hold of me with her eyes and I moved about a bit and she followed with her eyes. After some time she slowly started to wiggle and worked her way up to a cry. Eilis came in and looked at her and said, "You'll have to wait a minute until I get things ready."

Eilis then came in and lifted Aisling who at this time was crying loudly but not desperately. As soon as she was lifted Aisling stopped and gave Eilis a big wide smile and listened as she spoke to her. Eilis fed Aisling from the least preferred breast and she sucked loudly but then she started to let go and "mess", as Eilis called it, and so she sat Aisling up to get up her wind. Some sick came up and Eilis said that the boys were still running out of the room when the baby got sick. Eilis changed Aisling's's nappy and tried her again on the least preferred side again she started to "mess". When Aisling was upright this time, she got sick again on her cardigan. Eilis got another from her changer bag and put it on. Aisling was calm for this. As time was running out before their departure, Eilis put Aisling to the preferred breast and she was feeding intently as I left.

Visit six

10 am on 26 February

40 days

Eilis looked tired when she answered the door and quite different to the made-up and chirpy person who had answered the door the previous week. When I went into the sitting-room Aisling was sitting in her chair facing away from the window. She was asleep. She had her head tilted to one side and her hands were down by her sides. She occasionally fanned her left hand. Eilis told me that her worries about Aisling being colicky had been confirmed and that she had screamed for three-and-a-half hours the previous evening from five until after eight. Eilis told me about Donal who was colicky and Gavan who had had a condition called intussusception. Eilis said that she herself was in a distraught state by the time that Mac came home that evening.

Aisling continued to sleep as Eilis spoke to me, letting out occasional noises like sighs or sobs, as though she was still upset or knew what was being said. Eilis said that Aisling had had a good night's sleep after the crying incident but that she was sure that it was colic as she had had a very hard stomach and all Eilis could do was walk her up and down the room which had made Eilis's back sore.

Eilis went out to do something and I sat on the floor to watch Aisling. She moved her head back so that her chin was in the air. She licked her lips and pursed her lips into an "O" shape. Eilis came back in and turned the carry-chair around so that I could sit up on the sofa. After some minutes, Aisling's breathing changed and then she began to change her position now and then. Her left hand continued to move occasionally while her right hand was tucked up close to her body and the hand was covered by her cardigan sleeve. Eilis came in and said that they were going out to coffee at a neighbour's house that morning. She was looking at a dressy pink baby suit as she said this. The telephone rang and Eilis went to get it. Aisling was slowly waking up as Eilis told "Nana" about the colic episode.

Aisling's breathing changed and she started to wriggle and to move her head from side to side. She opened her mouth and started to grimace. After some minutes she opened her eyes and looked at me intensely but calmly. After some time she looked to the light. Eventually she started to pull her left hand in and out to her face and rub her face with her fist. Then Aisling started to cry out loud. After a short time Eilis came in and said, "You'll have to wait a minute now girly 'til I get your things." Eilis went out and came back with the changer bag and the dressy suit for Aisling's visit to the neighbours. Aisling was calm and seemed to enjoy the freedom when Eilis took off her clothes to change her. Her legs look very sturdy and she has a long, strong-looking body now.

Eilis invited me to inspect Aisling's nappy rash which I said looked like it was improving and hasn't gotten any worse since she told me about the baby wipes not suiting Aisling. Aisling started to cry again and Eilis told her she'd have to wait 'til she got her clothes on or she'd be cold. Eilis hurried the dressing and then put Aisling to feed which she did immediately. I said that I'd have to go and would I come on

Friday, as I knew she was going away that weekend as was I. Eilis said to ring about an alternative time. Aisling was feeding as I left.

Visit seven

6 pm on 1–3 March

45 days (5.5 weeks)

When I arrived at the house, the door was open and there were a number of children including Aisling's three brothers in the front garden near the door. I rang the bell and Eilis called out to me saying to come in. Eilis was feeding Aisling on the sofa in the sitting-room. Aisling was feeding very very quickly and with strong sucks. I could see that she had grown and said that I was amazed to see a difference in such a short space of time. Her hair had gotten longer and her face is fatter and her eyes are bigger. Eilis agreed and said that she herself could see it. I asked about the colic and she said that she'd never been as bad again but that she had had two or three bad days following that day. Aisling fed for a further five minutes or so and Eilis said that she had become very good at feeding quickly and could empty her breasts really fast now. I commented that she did seem to be feeding very quickly. Aisling's whole face was moving and quickly. Eilis said that at this time of the day, having been out, she is quite thirsty. Aisling was still wearing the lower half of her pram suit.

After a little time, Aisling let go of the breast and started to latch on again but instead started to fidget. Her legs started to move and eventually she started to cry with a pain. Eilis sat her up and she looked around and at me in-between being gripped by a pain and with her legs going up. For a while she kept the same arm, the right arm, tucked up by her body and fanned the fingers of her left hand. Eilis had shouted to the boys to close the front door and they had ignored her. Pol came in and was reading *Twits* by Roald Dahl, on the other couch. Eilis asked him to go and get the door and when he was gone she said to me, "They'll be saying the oul' bitch but they're ignoring me all the time." She said that Gavan is being particularly bold and that she'd even heard Mac saying to Gavan this morning that he had done a lot of bold things.

I said that it was normal and maybe she remembered the others like that with new babies and she said that they'd been too young to notice and I said that Gavan had been the baby for the longest time. She said,

"I suppose." Aisling grimaced every now and then though Eilis was rubbing her and she stuck her tongue in and out all the time. She was looking at me and seemed to be half smiling whenever she could relax. Eilis turned Aisling around towards her and spoke to her and Aisling relaxed for a short while and seemed to be listening intently, looking at Eilis's face and moving her mouth like hers. She soon got another pain and let out a loud yell. Aisling's cry has changed and is much stronger and more persistent now. After a while Aisling threw up and seemed to be better for a little while. Donal came in and asked to hold her. Eilis fixed the cushions for him to be secure in the seat and fixed Aisling in his arms. She seemed very happy there for a few moments. Eilis said, "I love when someone else holds her and I can really look at her." During this time Aisling moved her gaze first to me for some time, then to Eilis, and then to the print on the sofa. I was struck by the increase in her head control and in her ability to attend to one thing at a time but to do this going from one object to another and back again. Aisling started to wriggle and cry again and Eilis took her back. She held her out from her body with her hand tight around her stomach. The younger boys came in looking for tea and Eilis asked Pol to switch on the kettle. I offered to switch it on as it would need also to be filled and Aisling's crying had become more serious. Eilis said, "This is nothing compared to that day but this is her time of day." She said "I think it is for all babies" and I said well it was for mine. Eilis then followed the boys out to the kitchen and I followed as she was carrying Aisling in one arm faced out with her hand across her stomach. Aisling had a serious but calm look but continued to stick her tongue in or out and dribbled or threw up a little as Eilis made the tea for the boys and coffee for us with one hand. When the tea was made, Pol said that he hadn't asked and wanted it after the orange he was in the process of drinking. Eilis said, "If you think I'm starting again" and "It's there when you want it."

Gavan started to walk off with a full cup of tea and Eilis was struggling with him with one hand and taking the cup off him while holding Aisling with the other. Eventually they settled in the kitchen and she brought her coffee to the sitting-room and I followed, watching Aisling with my coffee in my hand. As soon as she sat, Eilis had to put down the coffee and feed Aisling, as the change of position seemed to bring the pain back.

She started to shake her head at the breast though and to yell and groan at it. Eilis said sometimes it's just about changing the position and stretched Aisling over her knee. She gave her a soother and this seemed to help her relax. After some coffee and after Aisling had let go of the soother a few times, Eilis put her back at the breast (right and preferred). After a few mishaps and letting go, Aisling started to feed as strongly as when I'd come in. Eilis said that Aisling is getting very assertive and that she had gotten a few scratches. I said I had to go and Eilis said have a good weekend and I said you too.

Visit eight

9 am on 12 March

6 weeks and 5 days

Eilis looked quite tired when she answered the door. I had spoken to her on the phone to arrange an earlier time than usual and she said that she had been quite sad when she visited her sister because it is just over one year since her father died and because her sister is separating from her husband.

Eilis said, "Come in, I'm feeding her in here." She had put Aisling on the couch to answer the door and lifted her up to let me see her face before recommencing feeding her. Aisling has grown, gained weight, and is quite plump in the face. Eilis even pointed out that her fingers are fatter. Aisling's skin has broken out and her eyes are less wide behind plump cheeks. She just stared at me solemnly for the few seconds. When she started to feed, I remarked to Eilis that it was fast but not as fast as the last visit. She said that she is still better able to feed than the boys and she might be satisfied after seven minutes a side. I noticed that Aisling's hair seems to be changing and falling out. After about seven minutes she pulled away and started to "play" with the breast and then got quite annoyed. She seemed to have a pain and started to make "ggnning" sounds. Then there started a spiral of checking if she wanted to feed, winding her, and then checking did she want to feed again. Aisling seemed very confused and unsure as to whether or not she wanted the breast—craving it and being angry and frustrated with it at the same time.

Eilis seemed calm throughout and eventually came down on the side of treating this situation as one in which Aisling had a pain rather than that she was hungry. She held her tummy firmly and talked to her with her face about one foot away. Aisling gave a few crooked smiles between yelling with the pain. I noticed and remarked that she now makes much more sophisticated movements with her hands involving single fingers. Eilis said she has beautiful hands and remarked that, "It's great when you get to know them—she's going to do something I can feel her tummy." Aisling got a bit sick and then did a noisy poo. She then smiled at Eilis and looked from one picture of the boys to the other as Eilis took off her clothes and she left her on the couch beside me as she went to get a bowl of water to wash her, etc. Aisling yelled loudly after a few minutes and I popped in the soother that Eilis had put beside her. When Eilis came back I moved to the pouffe so that Eilis could wash her. As she did she said, "I haven't seen you since her six week check—she did very well, she's gained three pounds, she's now eleven pounds."

Eilis also reported that she had taken Aisling to the doctor for her nappy rash. The cream he had prescribed had not worked and she stopped using it. It was improving now anyway. Aisling started to cry hard halfway through and Ellen put her nappy on quickly and tried her on the left where she wouldn't settle well. She got sick three times and Eilis said "Your Mammy's a joke" while cleaning the sick with the old clothes. When she spotted that there was poo on them, Eilis put soother in her mouth and went out to get clean clothes. Aisling continued to be unsettled when the soother dropped out and then dressed Eilis, put her back on the right breast where she settled into serious feeding, and that is where I left her. During the visit Eilis told me of instances of how "with it" Donal is, where Pol, though academic, is dreamier and can't always see things that need to be done in the way that Donal can. She said of Donal that "He's been here before" and that he knows how all the gadgets in the new car work.

Visit nine

8.30 pm on 16 March

7 weeks and 2 days

I telephoned to see when I'd come, as the family was going away, and Eilis said, "You can come now if you want, it's been a terrible day." She said that Mac was away and asked me to knock on the window. When I got to the house I forgot to knock on the window. Eilis let me in. She had Aisling facing out with her arm tight around her. I had heard her screaming on the telephone. She wasn't screaming now. Eilis shouted up to the boys to keep quiet but then went to go up and met them on the stairs. Once they saw who it was they went back. When Eilis brought Aisling into the sitting-room she sat down and started to rub her and stretch her. Aisling seemed fatter again and I said, "Well it's not interfering with her feeding anyway." Eilis had said on the phone that she'd been screaming since half past four in the morning and that she felt so sorry for her. Eilis walked up and down the floor. I said "You must be exhausted" and she said that it was hard also because Mac was away.

Aisling was going into sporadic episodes of contorting her body and screaming, then she'd yawn or roll her eyes and it seemed that if she did not have the pain she would be asleep. Eilis then sat down and said "I'll try but I think there's nothing left", and then a few minutes later said she was surprised that there was. Aisling relaxed and her skin calmed down and I noticed that her rash had gone and Eilis mentioned it as I was looking. Even though Aisling cried strongly while I was there, Eilis talked about it as though it was over. I said, "At least you'll get your sleep tonight." Aisling relaxed but still had her fists clenched. Eilis said that she was thinking of having a gin and tonic, and that perhaps I would also have one. Then she said that she was so tired that it would knock her out and opted for a coffee which I joined her in as a G and T was not an option as I was driving. Aisling lay parallel to me looking at the pictures and making a "gning" sound with her soother. When the soother came out I stuck it back in. Eilis came back with the coffees and took Aisling up and started to tell her and me about how she felt when the baby was crying. Aisling drooped and copied the mouth shapes and smiled between yells. Eilis and I then talked about plans for the Easter break. Eilis told me of her sister coming for Aisling's christening over the Easter break. They'd be there on my next visit. Aisling developed hiccups and Eilis talked about having felt Aisling's hiccups when she was still in the womb. She started to yell and Eilis sat her upright and rubbed hard—Aisling burped and got a bit sick. Eilis says that Mac claims that she cries when he takes her. Aisling started to roll her eyes and to roar and with her body and arms and legs agitating. Eilis started to feed her on the right and I said I'd go and then sat for a moment on the other couch when Eilis asked me about the arrangements for the next visit and we agreed it.

Visit ten

9 am on 24 March

8 weeks and 3 days

Eilis opened the door and asked had I phoned already and I said I had not as I was putting my bag into the boot of the car. Eilis said, "She's in here" as we went into the sitting-room. She said, "Wait 'til you see her, she has a cold." Aisling was in her chair asleep with the soother in her mouth and was sucking it even though asleep. Her nose was blocked and her breathing was noisy. Eilis told me that she had had a cold for a few days and that she had gotten a fright with her in the supermarket when she went really pale and she had to go very close to see if she was breathing. I commented that her skin is very fair although she is dark-haired.

Eilis told me that she had given Aisling a bottle and she was delighted that she had guzzled two ounces. She said that she had to go up to the north to pick up her sister who was coming down for Easter. They would all be there for Aisling's christening. Aisling continued to sleep. Her left hand was tucked into her cardigan. After fifteen minutes or so she let the soother fall out of her mouth and a process began of her turning her head from side to side, for a time sucking a phantom soother, and her eyes opened slightly and moved under closed lids. I called to Eilis in another room, asking would I put the soother back in and she said, "No," as she wanted her to wake up. Eilis came back in and we watched as Aisling slowly woke up and started a strong yelling. Ellen said that she had had a hard night as she could not suck her soother because her nose was stuffed. She had tried a saline solution, butter and sudocreme, which had worked.

Eilis cleaned Aisling's eyes before feeding her and Aisling accepted this. She fed hungrily and noisily. She had to pull away at regular intervals as she could not feed and breathe well at the same time. At one point the milk squirted upwards in an arch and Eilis commented that Aisling had made a lot of milk. Aisling continued serious feeding for another five minutes. Then Eilis cleaned her eyes again and her nose and changed her nappy and Aisling watched me a lot while Eilis did this. Eilis said, "Oh, she's not interested in me—she is saying, who is this new person?" After five minutes Aisling looked at the ceiling and then out of the window and eventually at the pictures of her brothers. Eilis chastised herself that she was a disgrace as she said that she had tried to make a print of Aisling's hand and she had not managed but that now Aisling had paint under her nails. I noted how elegant Aisling's hands are and how her nails look perfect, as if manicured. I asked if the boys were still mad about the baby and Eilis said just Gavan who had now settled out of a naughty phase and who still gives her hugs and kisses. Eilis sat Aisling up and she burped and was sick a little. Then she changed her clothes. I asked Eilis if Aisling was finished feeding and she said that she would feed her on the other side also as, although it was not easy, there was a lot of milk there. Eilis started Aisling on the left side where she "messed" (latching on, letting go, looking around, shaking her head) at first but then settled to serious feeding.

I said that it was time for me to go and Eilis and asked herself what time is it, saying that she also had to watch the time. I got the time of the next visit wrong and had to phone a few minutes after leaving to correct my mistake.

Visit eleven

9 am on 1 April

9 weeks and 4 days

Donal answered the door to me and there were two girls in the hall and then Eilis came down stairs with Aisling. Eilis suggested that we go "in here" and we went into the sitting-room. Then Eilis turned and introduced me to her nieces Emily and Helen. I said hello to the girls and we all went into the sitting-room. Eilis popped Aisling quickly into her seat and we both sat on the couch and looked at her. Her eyes were open and she was quiet. Her face has filled out and she has grown. Eilis said that the morning is her quiet time and that she will probably sleep, she had been fed at eight o'clock in the morning but she would probably feed her again. Aisling looked at the pictures and at the other children and to the noise coming from the television. Donal, Gavan, and the two older girl cousins were watching the television and Pol was stretched out on the other couch reading a book.

Then the youngest of the cousins came in sucking a soother and Eilis asked her would she like some breakfast and then asked Donal to get it for her. Donal and Gavan had been conspiring in whispers to do with "April Fool" pranks they were planning. Eilis said that Aisling has started to join her hands and I commented that she could also turn her head right around. Aisling had increased her level of movement and as a result Eilis said that she would feed her. She lifted her and Aisling fed intently on the right side for four to five minutes before falling asleep. Eilis said that she was not sure if Aisling was finished as she put her back into her tilted-back chair and put her soother into her mouth. I noted that there is a red hue in Aisling's dark hair and her hands are now dimpled.

Eilis said that she was having a coffee and asked me if I would like one too and I said that I would. Aisling started to wake up while Eilis was out of the room and Donal came over and put her soother into her mouth. Aisling blew it out again shortly afterwards and I called to Eilis would I put her soother back in and she said, "No," as she wanted her to wake up.

Eilis came back with Rice Krispie buns leftover from Gavan's party. She said that it had been bedlam at the weekend and that she had stayed up talking to her sister until 5am. She was looking forward to all the children going back to school next week. Aisling had gone quiet as soon as Eilis had started to speak, as though listening. Eilis took her up when she began to grumble. She put her on her knee facing her with her legs towards her and her head leaning away but facing her.

Aisling looked around at me for a while but spent most of her time craning her neck to see the others over her head and to the left. She looked at the TV and at the other children. I commented that she can swing her head right around now and Eilis commented that she can almost sit up when straining to see something. I asked had Aisling again had the pallor that had worried her and she said that she had—in the supermarket, in the same place, and that she then wondered about the light there—but she had had her sister with her this time and she had agreed that she had gone snow-white. Eilis seemed less concerned about it now. I suggested again that it might have something to do with her colouring and she said that she is going to have a tough job on holiday this year protecting Aisling from the sun.

Aisling had been still and looking around during this and now she started to wriggle and yell and Eilis put her to her right breast. Aisling must have had wind, as she continued to kick with her right leg. Eilis said that she loves when Aisling puts her hands up on her breast and while feeding and that Aisling looks at her more while feeding now.

Aisling continued to fuss and not to feed properly and Eilis sat her up very straight on her knee. She said that Aisling likes to be sat very straight to be winded and that she is glad that she does not bring up as much when she burps now. Aisling looked at me for a long while but mostly she looked around the room in a very intentional way. Eilis changed her nappy as Aisling relaxed and looked around her. Eilis dressed her in a lovely yellow cardigan and Eilis said that Nana's sister had made it for her for Easter. Eilis told how Mac had forgotten to get a roll of film in preparation for the christening. She put Aisling to feed on the left breast where she fed seriously after first fidgeting for a while and then fell asleep.

Visit twelve

9 am on 9 April

10 weeks and 5 days

Eilis opened the door with Aisling in her arms. Aisling was awake, looking at me and a little subdued. We went into the sitting-room. Eilis said, "I've just changed her, she was filthy." Aisling was in her vest and long woolly socks. Eilis was putting a white babygro and cardigan on her. I said, "How is she?" and Eilis said, "Oh, she's great" and then, "What am I saying, she's not great at all, in fact she's sick and on an antibiotic." Eilis said that Aisling was also on a cough bottle and that she had had to bring her to the doctor on Sunday when she was unusually quiet and sleeping more than usual. She had a chest infection and the cough would take some time to go.

Eilis went out of the room and Aisling was blowing bubbles through her mouth and was snuffling and congested in her nose. While Aisling was having her clothes changed she was able to arch her back, almost able to turn over on her tummy and her movements were so energetic and strong with her hands and arms going all over the place. Eilis had said, "Oh, look," when she did this and Aisling grinned at this. Aisling had also quietened to her mother's voice while faced away when being dressed and she smiled.

In her chair, Aisling looked at the wall tiles and at me and the observer role was reversed for some time in this way. Eilis came back with coffee for both of us and she gave Aisling her soother and as she did this she said, "She doesn't have it at night." Eilis went out again and Aisling lost the soother and went to nudge it back in off her chest with her two hands and almost managed. Eilis gave Aisling her medicine—she made faces especially for the cough mixture which Eilis gave her using a pipette. Eilis put the soother back in Aisling's mouth and Aisling started to yawn and get ready to sleep. Eilis put a heavy blanket over Aisling who took out her left hand and grasped the blanket on the outside.

Eilis went to put out the bins and Aisling sucked strongly on the soother and then this began to get quieter. I could hear the rattle in her chest and she sighed occasionally, she continued to look at the tiles and her eyes began to narrow—I notice that her eyes are turning darker now. Eilis came back and she made comments about Aisling as we watched her settle to sleep, needing the soother to be reinstalled three times. Eilis referred to the light parts of Aisling's now dark hair as orange at one stage and as copper at another. In the process of falling asleep Aisling made fleeting facial expressions changing every second. At first these were smiling expressions with a dimple appearing and disappearing on Aisling's right cheek and then they were more like pain or anger (or anger at feeling pain) before finally she began sleeping.

As Aisling slept, Eilis tells me that Aisling's nails are filthy and she hasn't had a bath since she got the cold five days ago. Eilis says that the day before, Aisling had worn her first dress. When she went to the school Donal brought two of his friends over to show them that his sister was wearing a dress and Eilis heard Pol on the phone to his Nana saying that Aisling was wearing a dress. Then Eilis said, "No, it wasn't the first time," that she had one for her brother's fortieth birthday party but no-one knew as Aisling had slept through this. Eilis said that she had in fact realised that she had put that one on backwards but it was the first real outward sign that Aisling is a girl.

Eilis said that everyone in the house had had the cold and that she had brought Mac to the airport and she doesn't know how he does it—going on a stuffy plane and than having to perform when he gets there—she couldn't be bothered.

Eilis said that she had fed Aisling before I arrived and that the feeding is going very well and that she hopes to continue feeding until after the holiday, when Aisling will be six months old. Eilis said that Aisling was turning twelve weeks old.

Eilis started to talk about Aisling being big for her age and then about Pol who is going to be nine on his next birthday and I said that I was thinking of him as nine already and that he is very big.

Eilis said that Donal was the only one who was small and slight. He was seven pounds and twelve ounces, Aisling was the second smallest at eight pounds exactly, Pol was nine pounds six ounces, and Gavan was nine pounds three ounces. Eilis told me how she had asked to see the afterbirth with all the children. This had started when she had agreed to take part in research with Pol and they were comparing the effects of different methods—the use of oxytocin versus the manual encourage-ment of the coming away of the afterbirth. The nurses that time measured the time it took to come away, checked its colour and condition and made sure that it was all there. Eilis noticed that for all but Donal the afterbirth was big and liver-coloured but for Donal it was small and grey as if there was a membrane on it. Aisling's was big and the nurses looked at Eilis as if she was mad when she asked to see it. She also said that the chords were surprisingly big and heavy. I said I suppose you were using it as an indication of how things were for her in the womb. She said she was and I said, "And you must have been doing okay to think of asking."

She said yes but referred to the fact that she hadn't any interest when Mac offered to video as they had before and they didn't protest when the nurse took Aisling away and washed her before the video which wasn't the original intention. Eilis said again that the birth wasn't nice.

As we were watching her, Aisling continued to sleep. Eventually she let the soother drop out of her mouth and Eilis said that at night she doesn't need it but during the day she will stick her thumb and almost half her hand into her mouth, so she sticks the soother back in if Aisling loses it even though she knows that if she's going to suck her thumb then there's not a lot to do about it. Eilis commented that the weather was so nice the day before that they had spent the day in the garden and she had done the housework when the kids were in bed. Eilis said that she'd been eating healthily since Easter and had lost three to four pounds. As I left, Aisling was sleeping, sighing every now and then. She looked a little "weak and watery" with her cold.

Visit thirteen

9 am on 16 April

11 weeks and 5 days

Eilis phoned the evening before my visit to let me know that she had to bring Aisling to the doctor the next morning and to cancel if needs be.

I said that I'd come ten minutes early so that she would be in time for the doctor's clinic.

When I got to the house Eilis saw me arrive and left the door open and shouted that Aisling was in the sitting room. Aisling was asleep on the couch with the right side of her face a bit buried in the cushion. She had her soother in her mouth and was sleeping uneasily with short breaths. A few minutes later she started to twitch and jerk all over and her eyes were moving inside her lids as though she were dreaming. She then started to fall into a deeper dream and the soother would start to fall out of her mouth and she would try to suck it back in. She fanned her left hand and as she started to relax it would go back down. She smiled in her dreams sometimes. Eilis gave me a coffee and went about doing the laundry. She showed me a dress that Aisling got for her christening. Eilis told me that Aisling now has rice with fruit in the afternoon, which she devours. She says that Aisling is less inclined to put her hand in her mouth and Eilis figures that she is getting a tooth on the bottom as she can see a white spot. I said that that would not help her chest infection and Eilis said that Aisling could not avoid the cold as everyone in the house has it and I note that Eilis has a hoarse voice herself.

Because she was going out, Eilis picked Aisling up as she had started to wake. Although she was still asleep, Aisling started to feed strongly and did so for about seven minutes. She woke up gradually and was then fully awake and gave huge smiles and I smiled back—it was impossible not to. I sat back and said, "I'm not supposed to be doing this, it's not part of the observer role but it's impossible not to she has such twinkling eyes," and Eilis said, "Yes she's beautiful." Eilis said that Aisling's ears have changed and she is going to have tufty hair like her uncle Michael. Eilis said that all of Mac's family are very nervous of choking and Mac gets very frightened of Aisling's cough. Aisling started a very bad cough just as I was about to leave, which followed the pattern of coughing after a feed. As soon as she stopped she started to smile again. I said goodbye and Eilis said that she would be out the door after me.

During the visit, Eilis said that she had had a period which she thought unusual as she was breastfeeding and I said that I knew lots of people that it had happened to. She said that she wished she was in work so she could organise a test of Aisling's sputum and know what organism it was. She also said she was upset about having given

Aisling the antibiotic. Eilis said she was also irritated at having to make a return visit to the doctors. It was clear that she was worried about her daughter's health.

Visit fourteen

9 am on 23 April

13 weeks and 5 days

Eilis let me in and went upstairs, saying, "She's in there." I went in and Aisling was lying on the couch with her head half buried in the cushion. Eilis came into the room and I asked how she was and she said she'd had an x-ray and she's clear. Eilis said that she still had the cough but that it was much better. Aisling has folds of skin on her neck since she has started to take solids. Eilis told me that Aisling has rice and fruit every day now. Aisling was breathing clearly. Whenever the soother started to fall out of her mouth Aisling would wake and put it back—she had her fingers in the soother chain. I gave Eilis a baby bracelet for Aisling's christening and she looked at it, said it was lovely and set it on the piano. Aisling's fingers have fattened and there is a little dirt under the nails. Eilis said that she still hasn't been washed since getting the cold and she's using cream to clean her. Aisling's dark hair has distinctly red flecks and since it hasn't been washed, it is flat and lying close to her head. Eilis said that Aisling would have hair like Mac's brother's—like a brillo pad—and, though very different in colour, it would be strong hair with something of the texture of her own also. Eilis told me that they had been worried about Aisling as her nephew with cystic fibrosis had died at eight years. Eilis said that she was very annoyed, as it transpired that Aisling had bronchialitis and she was particularly upset that she had had two lots of antibiotics unnecessarily. She had phoned for the results and the person had just said that it was clear but she knew that it was bronchialitis. She said that Aisling may be getting fond of having bottles and may not need the closeness of being fed. She said that the last night had been a bad night—the only bad night and that Aisling had wriggled all night without waking fully. Aisling was also wriggling now and arching her back and tapping her right toe. There was a noise outside and Eilis said, "Every time I hear that it reminds me of my bins." I said my goodbyes as it was time to go.

Visit fifteen

9 am on 30 April

14 weeks and 5 days

Eilis had left the door open for me and shouted to me that Aisling was in the sitting-room. She herself was in the bathroom. I went in and Aisling was plumped up on cushions on the couch. She was wide awake and thrashing around with her arms and legs. Aisling has taken a noticeable growth spurt since the introduction of solids and her eyes are less prominent now since her face has filled out. She watched me watching her for a while, then she turned around to the cushion and back again, as if checking to see if I'd still be there. When Eilis came in, she started to tell me that Aisling was well now and that her cough was gone.

When Eilis started to thank me again for Aisling's bracelet. Aisling started to vocalise too and got really excited when we spoke to each other for a few moments. Eilis then spoke to Aisling for some time and Aisling "talked" back. I said, "She's talking a lot now," and Eilis said that Donal now speaks to Aisling like she, Eilis, does and he caught Aisling laughing at him the other day. Eilis told me that Aisling has had a bath and that she had managed to remove cradle cap from her head using a method given to her by Mac's mother. Eilis went out to do some chores and Aisling watched her own hand for a while. She lost her soother and stuffed her thumb and forefinger into her mouth and sucked strongly. Aisling gave her mother a big smile when she came in to check through her soother which I had reinstalled, as she had started to cry.

Eilis took Aisling up and tried to get her to feed on the left (non-preferred) breast. There was a certain amount of wriggling. Eilis gave up and switched her over saying, "I'm going to look a sight on the beach." Aisling fed for about seven minutes before Eilis sat her up, feeling that she had wind or that something had stopping her feeding. Aisling burped and then started a poo which took some effort and she went red and Eilis said, "Maybe we'll have to cut back on the food if it's this hard for you,"—and then, "But that's two days' supply."

Aisling enjoyed having her nappy off and did not object at all as Eilis changed her on her knee. She then had her clothes changed but liked being jostled about. She then fed again for a further two minutes or so. Eilis had to put Aisling's hands down so that she could latch on.

Occasionally Aisling stops feeding momentarily as if to say "hello" to Eilis. She looks up at Eilis for some seconds and then continues. Eilis put Aisling down on the couch where she started to go asleep and went to do some chores before going out—I said time to go and Eilis said see you next week.

I noted that in this visit Eilis used words like "great", "wonderful", and "perfect" about Aisling, and she said that she was really enjoying her, unlike when Gavan was a baby with the other two pulling out of her. She said that it wouldn't take much for her to have another. I jumped in with, "Then you'd have two small babies," and she said, "I needed someone to tell me that." Aisling is having two meals a day now of rice and fruit at twelve and six approximately. Eilis said that Aisling's red marks under her hairline and on her forehead haven't faded much and still get very red when she cries.

Visit sixteen

10 am on 5 May

15 weeks and 5 days

Eilis let me in and we went into the sitting-room where the boys were home from school and watching the TV closely. She was awake in her chair and facing away from the TV and towards the door. When I came in and sat in front of her on the couch, she gave me a big smile and did this with anyone who passed her by. Aisling was sucking her soother and when she smiles the little red marks come up also. Aisling was holding her hands in front of her and moving her hands up and down in front of her face and back to her body again. Aisling's whole body goes into spasm when she starts smiling at someone. Soon Aisling was wriggling her whole body as if trying to go to the toilet. Eilis said that Aisling had gotten her injections, the Hib on one side, and the three-in-one on the other, on the day before my visit. Whenever Aisling heard Eilis's voice or saw her pass by she'd look up and smile. Aisling lost her soother and Donal jumped away from the TV and put it back in her mouth when she started her "gning" sound. Eilis asked the boys what cereal they wanted for their breakfast and a few minutes later, when they were called, both Gavan and Donal gave Aisling a little greeting and a head rub on the way out. When they were coming back to the TV, Donal stooped and talked to Aisling again for another few moments and a few moments later she lost her soother again and he returned it to her. I said to Eilis when she came in that Donal was good at giving Aisling back her soother and she said that she thought that he is a very kind boy whereas Mac says that he just can't stand the noise. Then she said, "But it is that he really is a kind child." Aisling's hands still look very elegant and she is now using them a lot. She seems to have grown bigger and to have lost some of the chubby look she was getting from the solids. She continued to wriggle a certain amount and there is still no sign of teeth. Aisling was bubbling at the mouth and Eilis said that she does that for days at a time and then it stops and starts again. Eilis was passing in and out and Aisling watched her. She did some farting and seemed to get some comfort from that for some time and continued to smile at the boys as they went back and forth.

Eventually a low groan became a yelling and Eilis came in and said, "I think she's hungry." Eilis put Aisling up to the left (non-preferred) breast. Aisling continued to latch on and then let go, and latch on again. Aisling would lean right back, look up at Eilis and give her a grin and go back to feeding again. Eilis said, "This drives me mad because since the introduction of solids I'm quite full." Aisling wriggled for some time and then fed seriously for about three minutes. Eilis said, "I seem to have won the battle this time." Aisling was then transferred to the right where she fed seriously. Eilis said that Aisling can take a rest while keeping the nipple in her mouth on the right side but not on the left and that they'd had an awful day the day before—it had been raining and they had not been out and the boys were home all day. Eilis says that she is experimenting with a third feed but she needs Aisling to feed a little more than she has been in the last few days. I said that I would be back the same time next week.

Visit seventeen

9 am on 14 May

16 weeks and 5 days

Eilis opened the door and lead the way into the kitchen where she had been feeding Aisling her solids. Eilis introduced me to her brother-in-law, Thomas, who was there for Pol's communion the following day. Aisling was sitting in her chair on the kitchen table and Eilis was standing up feeding her. Aisling was having baby rice which was all over her face and also on her pink bib. She was happy to be fed and was jigging about, waving her hands, and stuffing her hands in after the food. Her tongue was coming out a lot and Eilis took this as a sign that Aisling was teething. Eilis pointed to the fact that Aisling has a sticky right eye and snuffles again but she does not seem worried this time. Aisling was able to rock the chair and later Eilis commented that she would have to start to strap her in. Aisling gave me smiles through her baby rice. She watched Thomas and Mac who stayed talking there for a while before going out. In that time Aisling's eyes were then moving about the kitchen and she smiled any time there was conversation. She has learned to hold onto and pull things and she did this with her bib when being fed and at two other times during the visit. We moved then into the sitting-room where Aisling had her eyes cleaned with a saline solution, her nose cleaned, eye drops put in, and her nappy changed. For all of this, and even whilst having her nose cleaned, Aisling stayed calm and seemed to like being jiggled about and put at odd angles. Aisling struggled a little for having her nose cleaned. Her hair is falling out and she is getting even darker hair. Eilis checked that she'd told me that Aisling had had her "jabs" (vaccinations) the week before and had no ill effect. Eilis went to feed Aisling on the left side but she just cooed up at her and didn't settle at all.

Then Eilis sat her up on the edge of her knee facing out and Eilis's sister Grainne came back in and we were talking for a while and Grainne went out again. Aisling watched it all intently. Grainne left the room and Eilis then put Aisling on plumped-up cushions and then later on the flat on the couch while she went out to do the bins. Aisling was able to look at the back of the couch and then swing back to look at me or at what was happening in the room. I notice that Aisling can almost roll and almost turn onto her side now. She seems to get a lot of pleasure from being able to move her body and she pulls her legs right up and looks so eager as if she'd love to run around the room exploring everything. She was very pleased with the high vantage point on Eilis's knee. Grainne came back into the room and Eilis went past her to clean out the fireplace. When they started to speak, Aisling was first very excited and then stilled, as if listening to her mother in stereo.

When she was finished cleaning the fireplace, Eilis held Aisling up again on her knee, facing out. She seemed to be very pleased to see everything and when Mac and Thomas stood in the doorway to arrange jobs to be done with Eilis and Grainne, the baby looked from one face to the other and seemed to be attempting to follow the conversation and enjoying the raised level of activity. Aisling's nose was running and Eilis asked Mac to give her a tissue which he did. Eilis said that Aisling was almost at the point of sitting up and she let her back go for a few seconds to show me.

Eilis told me that the nights are a bit of a problem now and feels that Aisling may be comfort feeding at night for the feeds that she misses during the day since the introduction of the solids. Eilis said that Mac had to come out to give her the baby when she went to answer the phone one evening and that she had to bring her from room to room when tidying in preparation for her sister's visit—she wants to be with her more now. Aisling is eating her solids now with great glee. She has cereal in the morning, fruit and yogurt at lunch, and potatoes and vegetables at tea time. Eilis started to feed Aisling just before I went to leave because she had to go out and was leaving her with her sister. Aisling stopped after three minutes approximately and concentrated on a poo. Aisling "talks" a lot now, particularly when spoken to, and in general.

Visit eighteen

9 am on 21 May

17 weeks and 5 days

Eilis opened the door with Aisling in her arms facing out. She said "Come on in" and I followed her into the sitting-room where she was changing Aisling's nappy and putting her new clothes on her. Aisling has snuffles again. In her vest Aisling now looks tall and firm, not as pudgy as she was. Her face is big and different and her hair is falling out in tufts and seems to be being replaced by dark hair although her lashes are darker still. I followed Eilis out into the kitchen where she made us coffee with Aisling facing out on her hip. Aisling really loved this and her eyes were busy taking things in. Eilis again talked about the fact that the mark on her hairline hasn't faded. Aisling gave me a few smiles as I came into view but was intent on moving her arms and legs against the movement of Eilis as she was involved in dressing and changing her. Eilis said, "It's cold again and she has a cold again, I'm going to make sure that she's warm," and she put on two layers of clothes. Eilis held Aisling opposite her between garments and said that she'd had a big bowl of "Ready brek" and she said that Aisling is doing an awful lot of singing now. Aisling started to sing and Eilis put Aisling into her chair, sucking her soother and facing me. Aisling's new trick is pulling things—she pulled her bib. She also joins her hands again and puts them up and down. Eilis said that Aisling had had a lot of "Ready brek" and must be ready to go asleep. After Eilis put Aisling in the chair, she looked around the room. Eilis went to do things upstairs and in ten minutes Aisling worked herself up from gentle wriggling to full-blown crying and a distressed state—it was obvious that she had a bad pain in her tummy.

Eilis came back and picked Aisling up and this was the first time in a long time that I've seen her in a bad state. Eilis eventually started to walk about with her and, since she was tired, any time that she got any relief, Aisling started to close her eyes. She became quiet with her tummy on Eilis's shoulder and then the pain seemed to get bad again and Eilis walked up and down the room again. At one stage she distracted Aisling by something on the mantelpiece and Eilis faced her out from her and she was able to reach towards the card on the mantelpiece and then, when her hand rested on it, she was able to bring her other hand up and seemed to be playing with the feel of it on her fingers. This amused her for a few minutes and Eilis sat down and started to rub her back. A burp was then was followed by some smiling and talking to Eilis before another pain gripped her. Crying persisted so that Eilis said "Maybe you are hungry" and she tried Aisling on the right breast where I left them with Aisling feeding and falling asleep.

Visit nineteen

9 am on 28 May

18 weeks and 5 days

The door was open and the boys were about to go out when I arrived. The sun was shining and I went into the sitting-room where Aisling was on the couch with a light white blanket over her. Eilis popped her head around the door to see if I wanted coffee and I said everyone in this house is brown except Aisling. Eilis said, "You should see Pol," and she called him in and said, "Look at that," and threw her arm around him and gave him a squeeze, which pleased him. The four of them made a picture in the door frame as I looked out for a moment. Aisling was on the couch waving her arms and kicking her legs in the blanket. She smiled and made bubbles every time someone went by. She had no soother and pushed her hands into her mouth a lot. She would look at me for a few moments, then at things around the room and became quiet at hearing the voices of her family outside the room, listening. Eilis left her there most of the visit and came in occasionally to whoosh her up when she had slid down.

Aisling then started to shout and then came a song. She spent some time looking at her hands and sticking them in her mouth again. Eilis came in then and jiggled her about which she liked in the course of changing her nappy. Eilis then went out for a while and came in again and fed Aisling her breakfast in her chair. Aisling's spoon-feeding skill has gotten a bit better and the spoonful is eaten in three rounds of scrapping the food from around her mouth rather than five! She likes to hold onto her bib and to swing it about while being fed. Gavan came in and kissed the baby and Eilis said he could pick what she'd wear. He brought down two things which were discussed and discounted and the third was put on her after her breakfast. Eilis told me that she might be back at work for two weeks. She says that Mac had said it'll be good to know what it'll be like before the holidays. I left as Eilis was discussing Pol's bike with him at the door.

Visit twenty

2.30 pm on 4 June

19 weeks and 5 days

I was about to drive off when Eilis arrived back to the house from work saying sorry and that she was late—she was at work and hated it. Aisling had been sitting happily in the front seat facing back. Eilis dropped her into the sitting-room for me to observe and went to a house a few doors up the street to pick up the boys. Aisling sat and looked at me every now and then, giving me big smiles that made her whole body tense. She waved her arms and feet and started to talk to me. She looked around the room, gave me a big smile—she did this in cycles. Eilis came back with the boys and started to respond to various demands they were making. She said that Aisling was due a feed but she spent some time singing before the demand came into Aisling's voice and she began going red a few times. I thought that she would dirty her nappy. This was the first time that I refused coffee. Aisling fed for five minutes strongly on the right. Eilis commented that she smelled lovely and her skin was soft. "I don't know what your granny has been putting on you," she said. Eilis said she did not want to put the granny under pressure by asking her to hold off with the feed. She sat Aisling up on the edge of her knee and showed her body control and she also showed her sitting for a few seconds unsupported. Eilis told me of Aisling's singing and she noted that the boys aren't interested in her as much. She told me Mac was away and recounted her exhausting itinerary of the previous day when they all went first to town and then to a shopping centre after work, getting home at about half past nine in the evening.

Aisling waved her hands and brought them up to her mouth. Her mother put her first on the floor and she turned from side to side arching her back—this was the first time I've seen this. Aisling stuck her hands into her mouth a lot. After some time, Eilis picked Aisling up to see if she was finished feeding. Aisling burped and Eilis sat her up facing me and showed how she liked to sit up. Then she tried Aisling on the left and she fed for seconds, then gazed up at Eilis for a time and then fed again. She just beamed up at Eilis and was taking the very occasional suck and Eilis decided that she was finished.

Donal came in and asked could he hold the baby and Eilis arranged him on the floor and gave him Aisling, arranging his hands around her and warning that she can jump. When Eilis took Aisling back she tried to feed her again and then Aisling started to fall asleep. Eilis took Aisling away from the breast and I commented that her eyes were closed as I left, saying that I'd come again at the same time next week but as Eilis will still be working I'd call during the week to confirm.

Visit twenty-one

3.30 pm on 12 June

20 weeks and 6 days

I had called on the previous day as arranged, knowing that Eilis was not going to be there if her mother-in-law wanted her to go shopping. They went shopping. I telephoned on the weekend to make another arrangement and Eilis reminded me that I would have only two more visits before they went on holiday. She said that I could visit any time before half past four, when they were going out. I called at about half past three.

Donal opened the door and said, "Come on in." Eilis was there with Donal, Gavan, and Aisling and she was feeding Aisling who was sitting in her chair while she, Eilis, was sitting on the couch. I said, "What's she eating?" and Eilis said that it was a mixture of yogurt and fruit—banana and kiwi. I said "She's better at eating now"—a spoon was gone in three goes. Aisling was very co-operative while having her nappy changed and hung her head over Eilis's knee. She was able to twist her head around to watch the boys watching TV. Eilis said, "Will we let you stand up?" and when she let Aisling stand on her knee, Aisling got very excited and went through moments of smiling, tensing her body, and being still, followed by a flurry of activity. Eilis then put Aisling on the floor and put a yellow rabbit over at Aisling's right hand at arm's length. Aisling started by tensing her body so that her back and bottom were off the floor. Somehow she managed to get herself over to the rabbit and then she worked herself away from it again. In the last few visits Aisling's body control and mobility have really taken off. She sang away to herself for these few minutes on the floor, then she began to shout as if telling someone off.

Eilis came in and picked her up. She sat over on the other couch with her, getting her to sit up on the floor for a few moments at a time, unsupported. Eilis said, "She's tired or maybe she wants a drink," and she tried to feed her. Aisling started to "mess", nodding her head around rather than latching on, and this coincided with Gavan and Donal coming into the room.

Gavan was walking up on the back of the couch beside them and he and Donal were also talking to Eilis. It occurred to me that there was too much activity for Aisling to concentrate on feeding. Eilis put Aisling alongside her on the couch where she watched and listened to the boys and then when Aisling started to give out again, Eilis tried to feed her again but she wriggled and wasn't interested. Eilis said she often does this when she's tired and needs to go to sleep. She likes to feed to go to sleep but she has to try her a few times. Eilis stopped trying to feed Aisling and held her on her lap for a while and they looked at a necklace together. It looked gold with diamonds in the middle of each piece and Aisling fingered it and examined its detail with a look of great concentration. There was a ring also and Donal was very interested in these and he had to try on the ring. Aisling also watched Gavan and Eilis and then the two boys in conversation and she looked from one to the other, depending on who was speaking.

There was lots of fun and games and Gavan then went into the kitchen to put on the radio to dance and Donal said, "He's closed the door because he doesn't want anyone to see him." Eilis laughed and said, "I don't know about these boys of mine—one wears my jewelry and the other likes to dance!" Donal went out to Gavan in the kitchen and he was running in and out reporting on Gavan and then went out and there was teasing going on between them. Aisling was very still and seemed to be listening to the boys. Eilis put her in her chair to go to sleep but she complained there and she took her out again and this time she fed strongly but only for about four or five minutes. Then Eilis put Aisling in her chair and got Donal to get her blanket while she rocked her. She covered her and installed her soother. Donal had taken down a polished stone that was in two pieces and Eilis got on the floor beside the boys and they were examining the stone. Aisling was watching this and her eyes were narrowing in sleepiness. They were trying to decide what kind of stone it was. Eilis asked me what I thought it was and I said that I hadn't any idea. Just as it was time for me to go Aisling had closed her eyes and her head was relaxing to one side as I left.

Visit twenty-two

9 am on 18 June

21 weeks and 5 days

Eilis answered the door and told me that Aisling was in the kitchen, as she went to get Aisling a bib. Aisling was in her chair on the kitchen table. Her hair has mostly fallen out and the new hair is short and dark. Aisling was in good form and rocking herself in the chair. As she began to feed her, Aisling was eating very quickly and Eilis said, "I've never seen her so good at eating her breakfast." Aisling was holding Eilis's jumper sleeve as she ate. She was looking at Eilis and chatting, singing, and talking whilst also eating her breakfast.

Eilis talked about how she has felt under pressure these last few days, getting the clothes packed etc. for going away for the four-and-a-half weeks. She said that Mac doesn't have to think of any of it and then quickly said that she can leave the driving and the money to him, so it balances. Eilis said that Aisling's sleeping has settled again. We then went into the sitting-room as the nappy-changing bag was there.

Eilis talked of how the boys were excited and went happily to school that morning with bread and yogurt for lunch and no bars and yet they didn't care, whereas there would usually be a row about the lack of bars. As Aisling was having her nappy changed she was completely relaxed, looking around the room with her head hung over Eilis's knee and her whole fist stuck in her mouth. Aisling was able to lift her head up occasionally using her tummy muscles to see Eilis. I said that I hadn't seen her with her whole hand in her mouth like that before and Eilis said that she does it a lot and she even has her fingers in sometimes when she's feeding. She said that she was so addled that she was writing all the places where they were going to for her brother but she wasn't sure whether she had already sent him a copy or not.

She was also doing a shopping list for Mac's mother. I had the feeling that since Eilis's own parents are gone, her mother-in-law has taken their place in some ways. She said that they would have their lunch with Mac's parents on the way to the boat. She said that the previous day she hadn't enough milk when she went to feed Aisling and so Aisling had had a bottle in the middle of the day. I commented that the walker was new and Eilis said, "Yes," and that a friend had loaned it to her and Aisling loved it because she can stand up in it. Eilis said, addressing herself to Aisling, "And you're getting teeth." I asked had she seen one and she said no but that Aisling has been sticking her tongue out a lot and drooling. Eilis said that Aisling has a strangely shaped mouth that is hard to see into. She said to Aisling, "Now we'll show off your standing up in a moment."

Eilis put Aisling on the floor and went to get coffee. Aisling stretched out her left hand and tried to pick at the textured flowers on the rug. She then played with her left toes with her left hand. As Eilis came in she commented that Aisling was reaching and grasping more now. The doorbell rang as Eilis put the coffee down and as she didn't react I said that the doorbell had rung. Eilis said that it was a sad case of what, in summary, might be referred to as a "latch-key child" left to his own devices. Eilis said she felt very sad going away and leaving him alone. Eilis answered the door and the little boy came in. She said sit down, making a space beside him and told him to take off his coat. Eilis put Aisling in her new walker and offered the little boy breakfast, speaking slowly as he could not understand easily. They went out and Eilis came back in and said that the little boy went to a private school but there was no "care". She said that she had left a note for another neighbour to say that she would be away. She commented that Aisling was turning the buttons on the walker. The phone rang and Eilis went to answer it.

Aisling had been standing in the walker and taking weight on her feet and getting the walker to go backwards. She now was jammed into the fire hearth and began to complain rather than sing, as she had been. The little boy arrived in with her soother which she sucked, putting her face on the tray of the walker every few seconds—I wasn't sure whether she was frustrated or tired. As the complaining got worse I heard Eilis tell the person on the phone that the baby was crying and saying goodbye.

Eilis took Aisling out of the walker and straightened the feet on the velour pink babygro that she wore with a cream chunky hand-knit. Either the rearranging of her clothes or being picked up made things a little better but Aisling persisted with a low "errr" complaining cry and Eilis tried to feed her. She fed for three minutes and then pulled away and cried. Eilis offered her again and she refused. Eilis took her away from the breast and snuggled her and she started to close her eyes. Then she transferred her to her chair as they were to go to the passport office after my visit and said, "We'll have to be going soon."

I looked at my watch and said "I'll go then" and Eilis said "I'm not going for another few minutes, if you're not finished" so I sat down again. Eilis rocked Aisling with her foot as she applied her make-up.

Aisling opened her eyes occasionally and the intervals were getting longer. She changed her head position from left to right a few times. Eilis said that it was a pity that they had to go out in the cold as she might wake up. I said that it was time for me to go and to have a great holiday. I said that I would phone as soon as they got back to make another visit before they set off again. Eilis had mentioned on the previous visit about her family having a reunion in Ireland when she got back from holiday. I smiled and said goodbye to the little boy as I let myself out and as I turned my car Eilis was getting Aisling into the car. I wondered what would happen to the little boy and how his situation was so starkly different to Aisling's. I noted that Eilis had made several comments during this visit suggesting that she was still totally besotted with Aisling.

Visit twenty-three

9 am on 26 July

27 weeks and 1 day

I had telephoned on the family's return from holiday to arrange my visit. Eilis answered the door and immediately went back to Aisling in the kitchen. Another woman was there in her nightdress—Eilis's sister -in-law. Aisling looked longer, neater, and she had tight dark hair with a red brown fringe, and two bottom teeth.

There was another baby there, Robert, who was very big for his eighteen months. Aisling was having breakfast on Eilis's knee and she moved continually. Then she went in her walker. Eilis said the holiday was great and that she had slept well and was "really good" on holiday—it was like being a young couple with one child because the boys played together. Aisling came over to me and looked at me and started to pick at the circles pattern on my trousers. Then she slobbered and mouthed my knee. She played with two balls that Eilis gave her and when she started to cry. Eilis said she may want a drink. She tried her at the breast and said very quickly that she wasn't bothered. Eilis played with her on her knee as I was leaving.

Visit twenty-four

9.30 am on 4 August

28 weeks and 1 day

Eilis answered the door. The house was full of children. Mac had come home the night before with presents for the children—his own children and visitors' children—including six feet of bubble gum each! Eilis told me news of her weekend away while Aisling sat on her knee and looked like she wanted to jump off, she jigged constantly. Eilis made no attempt to feed her and Aisling did not appear hungry throughout the visit although breakfast had been at six o'clock. She seemed to be beginning to get hungry at the end of the visit. The children were in and out and Eilis was watching them in horror as they munched their way through the gum. I met Thomas, Eilis's brother, and Mac seemed to have gotten up and was talking to Thomas in the kitchen towards the end of the visit. Eilis told me that she wasn't a bit nice to the kids on the few days they'd already had their holidays. I realised only at the end of the visit that, since Mac was still away, she had taken the children away on her own. Eilis offered me chocolate with kiwi which Mac had also brought home. She seemed to be quite relieved that he was back and said that she was exhausted.

Aisling was playing with a new toy that Mac had brought her, which was really interesting to her and absorbed her for some time. She is very precise in the way she uses her fingers now. Eilis put Aisling on the carpet and she was able to get to a lot of things on the floor by pivoting on her hands. Donal came in when I was on my own with Aisling and sat behind her as she sat on the carpet and put his arms around her and held her, which she loved. After some time he offered me to hold her and looked so alarmed when I told him that I couldn't that I called Eilis in on the conversation and she confirmed for him that it was alright, that I was observing Aisling and therefore couldn't hold her.

When Eilis took Aisling back up on her knee Pol came in and snuggled up to Eilis on the couch. Aisling was able to turn herself right around, look at Pol, and touch him. When Donal came back in and went up on the back of the couch she was able to turn around in the opposite direction to look at and smile at him. As I left, Aisling had been offered the breast and was not interested and was rubbing her eyes and Eilis was holding her close, which she does before she sleeps.

Visit twenty-five

9.30 am on 27 August

31 weeks and 5 days (7 months and 10 days)

Eilis answered the door and we went into the kitchen where Aisling was scooting around in her walker wearing a babygro suit with the feet beginning to wear and get grubby—I noted to myself that she was at the "impossible to keep clean" stage. I noted that any vestiges of the "new baby" look are gone and all this movement makes her seem more like a toddler. Eilis had also told me on the phone that the breastfeeding was finished and that Aisling wasn't bothered once she got used to the formula. Aisling is on four bottles a day now. She had been having her breakfast and scooting at the same time and when I sat she took some time to investigate the buttons on my skirt and contemplated putting one in her mouth before she decided to go further afield in the walker. When breakfast was finished, Eilis went to do things in the other end of the kitchen and Aisling got frustrated after a time and shouted until Eilis came and nudged her walker over the lip dividing the boards at the dining end from the tiles at the sink/cooker end of the kitchen.

When Aisling started to give out about the restriction of her movement Eilis took her out saying, "Wait 'til you see her crawl." Aisling didn't crawl but pushed her head against the walker and bottom-shuffled.

Then she pushed the walker away from her and looked at this thing, the walker, which she had spent so much time inside, from a different perspective.

During the time in which her clothes and nappy were changed Aisling was in perpetual motion. She seems unbelievably motivated to be mobile. Eilis told me about her plans for going back to work and her arrangements for having the children minded. She showed me Aisling's inverted nipples and said that a niece who'd been there on a visit last summer also has them. Then she said "Of course, none of the boys have them, it would have to be her". Eilis told me that she would be working fulltime for three weeks and felt sorry leaving Aisling with the minder all day as contrasted to half a day with two doting grand-parents. I made an arrangement to see Aisling in the evening for these three weeks.

Visit twenty-six

6 pm on 1 September

32 weeks and 2 days (7.5 months)

Eilis sat in the sitting-room with Aisling on her knee, watching Donal and Gavan across the road playing in a group of children. They were playing with cut grass. Mac had taken Pol to his football match. Eilis said she was "dead" with the long days at work but that the baby minder was nice and the boys were good with Aisling. Aisling had no nappy on and Eilis said, "Look she has a sore bottom; I'm letting the air at it." Aisling was in her arms and sitting on the edge of her knee as though she wanted to launch herself. She was smiling and contented but impatient to get going.

Aisling sat in the middle of the floor and could get at everything on the floor. Eilis went out of the room and Aisling tried to follow her but she had to try to crawl with straight legs as her dress was getting in the way and she started to yell out at Eilis who was saying reassurances in to her such as "Yes, I'm coming", etc. When Eilis came in and sat down and took Aisling up beside her on the couch, Aisling was happy and Eilis offered her a bottle but she didn't drink it and just played with it. Aisling had been up for an hour at four o'clock and Eilis said it could have been teeth, the change in routine, or the sore bottom etc., as she had her bottle. Aisling won't go in between them in the bed as the others did—she is not used to it. Eilis showed me the tadpoles which Mac brought back as dried eggs in a pack from his work trip.

Eilis thought they were disgusting—like shrimps. She said she told the kids that she was going to make stir-fry with them for a joke. Aisling started to get cranky and Eilis heated her bottle, as she doesn't like it cold. She said she'd like Aisling to take a nap of a half hour, and then she could have a bath and go down for the night. Aisling was getting a tight snuggle and her eyes were closed before I left.

Visit twenty-seven

6 pm on 7 September

33 weeks and 4 days

I called in as the door was open and Eilis said, "I forgot all about it." I went in and she was eating her dinner with baby on her knee, having the occasional forkful. Eilis said, "I'm just in the door." The others' empty plates were on the table and Mac had gone out with Pol. Eilis thought that Aisling looked pale and asked did I think so. Donal and Gavan came in looking for a chocolate spread sandwich and Gavan wanted an ice cream. They had just the cone wafers and Eilis put Aisling on the floor with one. Donal tried to embarrass his mother for not having ice cream. The boys went back out to play. Aisling started to mash the cone into the floor and listened to the crunch, then she ate the pieces.

Eilis made coffee for us and Aisling had a chocolate bar while sitting on her mother's lap. At one stage she started to choke and Mother gave her a drink of lemonade from a cup. She put Aisling on the floor again, where she started to pull to stand at Eilis's chair. Eilis started to clean up the kitchen and Aisling crawled around the kitchen. I asked if she was sleeping and Eilis said that there had only been one night that she had slept through since my last visit. Eilis's brother was on the phone and she had asked about his wakeful daughter, Sinead and they were "sick" of her. Eilis wondered if Aisling was going to be another Sinead. Eilis started to tap on the wipes box and Aisling pushed Eilis's hand back so that she would do it again when she stopped. They took turns and Aisling alternated hands—like piano playing—and Eilis said, "She goes mad when Mac plays the piano," and wondered if she remembered the sound from when she was in utero as, "he always plays the same kind of tunes."

Eilis went to unload the dishwasher and Aisling pulled herself up to stand at the dishwasher and started to take out the plates. Eilis then put her in the walker in order to finish the job and took her out again soon after when she made a mild objection. Eilis was carrying her around and tidying at the same time. I asked Eilis if she thought that Aisling was clingy since she'd been at work and she quickly said, "No, it's me. I wouldn't lift her like this if I were here all day. I know that I only have a few hours with her and that's why I don't mind her waking up at night. But it will be nice when I'm working two days and we can have our walks in the park in the mornings." I said it was time for me to go and Eilis walked out with me, with Aisling bright-eyed in her arms, to get the boys in.

Visit twenty-eight

7 pm on 14 September

34 weeks and 2 days (8 months)

Gavan answered the door and Eilis said, "She's asleep, I'm just in and apparently she's been crying all day." I went upstairs after Eilis and she said, "Sit on the bed," and pushed away some clothes so I could watch Aisling sleeping. She had her soother in her mouth and lay on her left side with her right hand over the covers. The hand moved every now and then and she sighed occasionally and sucked vigorously for a few seconds at a time. After about ten minutes she started to wake up and eventually did, sitting up towards the wall with a few cries that brought Eilis up, so that Aisling didn't know that she'd been alone with me. When she turned and looked, both Eilis and Gavan were in the room.

Eilis carried Aisling downstairs and she didn't really get upset in the waking process. Eilis held her and she played a game of grinning with Pol and Donal while on Eilis's knee. Eilis said, "Show Margaret your teeth," and got Aisling to clap also. Mac was there hearing the boys' homework. Aisling ate some bits of bread dipped in soup which Gavan fed to her with Eilis's permission.

Aisling then moved away from Eilis over to the pouffe where the boys were. She made everyone laugh by showing her bottom (only) teeth and then she played tapping, taking turns with Pol and Donal. Eilis knelt on the floor to ensure that if Aisling fell that she would not hit her head on the hearth. Donal asked Pol to move so as not to block my view. Aisling then started to crawl around the room. There was talk of Mac's travels for work and Eilis made coffee for the adults. Aisling came back to her to be picked up when she came back in. Mac said to Eilis, "If you weren't here she'd be over here with the boys." Una, Aisling's minder, had called to see whether she had settled after her upset all day. She had pink cheeks and rubbed her right ear. She was tired and covering her face as I left.

Visit twenty-nine

8.45 am on 24 September

35 weeks and 6 days (8 months)

Eilis let me in with Aisling in her arms. We went into the sitting-room and Eilis went on the floor with Aisling playing with her. Then she let her onto the floor to play—telling me about Mac being away. Aisling was looking at me with suspicion and was clinging to Eilis. She hadn't settled the previous evening for the babysitter when Eilis was absent for two-and-a-half hours. She had a runny nose and soother and was miserable. While Aisling was hanging onto her, Eilis said, "I think she's hungry." Eilis said Pol was delighted with himself that he was able to settle Aisling. Eilis said that she knew that he would. Aisling is sleeping better since Eilis is at home more. Aisling started to look warily at me again and Eilis took her up saying, "No wonder Mammy's got a sore back," and took Aisling out to the kitchen where she put her in her walker to give her breakfast. Aisling cried at being put in her walker and Eilis said, "And your feet are cold and I don't know where your shoes are." Aisling had a runny nose and was more upset than I've seen her, except for the "colic" episode. She had her eyes half-closed and came behind Eilis as she prepared her breakfast and bottle.

Eilis heard the neighbour at his bins and remembered hers and said, "She's going to roar but I have to do it." Aisling did and hid, first behind the kitchen door, and then the open press door furthest away. Aisling's eyes closed and she roared with big tears. I said, "No, no, baby," when the crying got very loud. Eilis came back in and said, "Look what I have for you," directing Aisling's attention to the "Ready brek". She called Aisling over to her, sitting down at the table near me and Aisling came over and was instantly calmed, concentrating on the food—she was very hungry. Eilis said, "You'll be crying of a pain in your tummy next," as she finished off the bowl of cereal. Eilis figured that Aisling had refused a bottle the night before with the sitter. Eilis had to dress Aisling quickly to bring Pol to the dentist and Aisling was clinging to her and hiding from me. Eilis joked, "If Margaret bites you I'll bite her back." Aisling has red and light brown streaks in her hair. My comment got the response, "Yes, she is gorgeous." As soon as she was dressed, Aisling snuggled into Eilis and made it obvious that she wanted to sleep. As soon as Eilis gave her the soother, she was asleep, and she held her for a few moments until she was sound asleep. Eilis then put Aisling in her buggy on her side with pyjama bottoms for a cover. Aisling jumped but didn't waken with the noise I made as I was leaving.

Visit thirty

8.45 am on 1 October

36 weeks and 6 days

When I arrived I told Eilis her window-box had blown over and she went out to fix it, and I went inside to Aisling who was in her walker and beamed a smile at me which was an altogether different reaction to the last visit. She was bright-eyed, her hair has grown, and she looks bigger. When Eilis came back, she followed her around trying to catch the toggle on her fleece top. She managed this a few times. Aisling spent much time pulling at Eilis's leggings and giving an occasional shout. Eilis said that Aisling stood for a few seconds by herself during the week. While being fed, Aisling played with a little digital toy with buttons and lights and sucked her hand along with her breakfast with such force that a lot of her face disappeared as she sucked in the food and her hand. Then she stretched for things as if the walker wasn't there, pulling several things off the counter tops. Aisling stood at the dishwasher as if unloading it. Eilis told of a harassment issue at work and at the same time dealt deftly with Aisling when she was choking in the middle of Eilis's story. Eilis said she would like more space in the house so that she could have her family to visit more comfortably.

Visit thirty-one

8.45 am on 8 October

37 weeks and 6 days

Aisling is in her walker during this visit. She was having her hands washed in the downstairs bathroom when I called. Eilis explained that it was in preparation for going to granny's. I noted a general air of tiredness from both of them. Aisling had bronchialitis again and coughed during the night. She followed Eilis around the kitchen, pulling at her trousers to be picked up and Eilis spoke of her sore back. Aisling had been to the baby clinic and was just over the correct weight for her age. Aisling was looking warily at me again and pulling at Eilis at the same time. She smiled at me once. Eilis gave her a crisp packet to play with and Aisling liked making noise with it. Then Eilis gave her a toy zebra and a rattle on her tray but she persisted with looking to be lifted. Eilis then gave her halved grapes which she ate with concentration and relaxation and with her back to me. Aisling made a demanding cry when Eilis went to change and so she came back as quickly as she could, buttoning her dress at the door, and lifted Aisling who cried and then settled when Eilis put her back in the walker to put on make-up, saying, "Don't moan." Eilis told me of Aisling's achievements—for example, she can find the remote control. Eilis also spoke of concerns about Mac's parents—she said that she thought Aisling would sleep in the car.

Visit thirty-two

9 am on 15 October

38 weeks and 6 days

Aisling was sitting on Eilis's knee in the sitting room—as she used to when little. This was because Eilis's sister was visiting. There were three other cousins visiting. Aisling seemed very happy and was climbing all over Eilis. The children were sitting quietly and Aisling would go away a little to explore and then come back to Eilis for a while. She then fell asleep on Eilis's knee. There was much talk during this visit which may have tired Aisling.

Visit thirty-three

9 am on 22 October

39 weeks and 6 days

Eilis was carrying Aisling in her arms as she answered the door to me. Aisling smiled at me as she contentedly allowed herself to be changed on her mat on the kitchen table. She had a runny nose and bronchialitis and Eilis said that she had gotten her incisors. Eilis says that she doesn't think that she will get Aisling's "jabs" (vaccinations) because Aisling is unwell.

Aisling cries and taps at the window to Eilis when Eilis has gone out to the back garden to prepare the bins for collection. Aisling makes silent mouthing shapes with her mouth and seems to be comforting herself. Aisling's eyes are heavy and more closed than usual. She followed Eilis on her return from the back garden, wanting to be picked up.

Then Aisling perked up and became engrossed in playing with the dishwasher right beside Eilis. Next, Eilis put Aisling in her highchair where she played with a ball, pills in a box, and pieces of apple. I noticed that she was really biting things. Aisling made a lot of faces while eating the apple. The atmosphere in the house that day seemed quiet and sad. Eilis reported that the house had been empty when she came back from a trip to a wedding. Mac is away. Even though she is sleeping well, Eilis notes that Aisling is clingy.

Visit thirty-four

10 am on 28 October

40 weeks and 6 days (9.5 months)

I called on a different day to suit Eilis's work schedule. Today Eilis was smiling at me as she opened the door. Aisling smiled at me and reached out her hand from her buggy. I commented that she looked taller and Eilis said it was the leggings. I put my hand over to Aisling and she grabbed it. She was strapped into her buggy and had her soother in her mouth. I asked if she was going to sleep and Eilis said, "Probably." Aisling was playing with the top of her bottle and there was milk on her hand. She started to cry and Eilis turned her so she could see her while she was doing the washing up. Eilis started to tell me that Aisling is really spoiled now and that she cannot put her down or she cries and her "back is broken".

Aisling has a bad cough and Eilis reports that she was sick all over herself in the night. Eilis showed me all the teeth that Aisling is getting at the same time. Aisling started to yell and Eilis carried her with her while making coffee. A little while later Aisling had to wait to be picked up. Whilst in her buggy, Eilis had told her, "You'll just have to wait." She said, "I know it's my own fault—but sometimes you just feel like telling them shut up, but then," and she seemed to think happier, fonder thoughts. Aisling was immediately happy when Eilis sat down and it was a little hard to concentrate on Aisling while Eilis spoke. She talked of Aisling's beautiful hair and hands and she cleaned her with baby wipes. Aisling objected very little. Eilis gave her a pencil case to play with and also the small digital toy. Aisling attempted to press the buttons on this and then took all the pencils out, one by one, and examined them individually. When she threw them on the floor Eilis picked them up and laughed that it was becoming a game. Aisling started to explore and climbed on Eilis's knee and Eilis shook her fist behind her head. She said, "I shouldn't give out, she's very good." Aisling was biting the chair and Eilis let Aisling chew her finger for a few seconds. The boys came in but Aisling stayed quietly on Eilis's knee. Gavan and Donal and friends were showing off what they could do with Halloween blood paint. The doorbell rang and someone groaned and answered it. A little girl from the neighbourhood came in to no acknowledgement. Eilis told me that she was deaf and that her parents had died and that she often came down to be with the boys whom she knew from school. Eilis admired Gavan's fake cut on his hand but not the little girl's as she held hers out too.

Eilis said, "I love you to death when you are asleep," to Aisling, and then, "I haven't had one evening when I could relax downstairs after they've gone to sleep—both of us jump if she is in bed because she might be sick if she coughs." Eilis was sounding unusually tired and Aisling was whingey and clingy. Just before I left, Aisling was looking to be put in her buggy, eager to expedite the "picnic trip" that was about to get under way.

Visit thirty-five

8.45 am on 5 November

41 weeks and 6 days (9.5 months)

Eilis opened the door saying, "Isn't that beautiful weather, she's in there, in that mess of a kitchen." Aisling was in her highchair with her soother in her mouth looking contented and not at all disturbed by my arrival. Aisling has a fatter face now and has put on weight. She went pink and I thought that she was going to cry but Eilis said "She's doing a poo". Aisling was holding a hairbrush which she was waving and soon dropped. She looked after it but forgot it then. She picked at the screwdriver slot in the screws in her chair. She looked from me to Eilis who was cleaning and talking. Eilis said that Aisling has gone off her breakfast and that she will have to think of something else for her. Eilis had to come over to Aisling a few times to wipe what she called her "snotters".

Aisling smiled at us in turn as she ate her breakfast. She was sucking in her face and waiting for a reaction. This sucking in her top lip is a new trick and she sang and jiggled as she ate. Eilis had to give Aisling her own spoon to hold as she was trying to grab the spoon and spilling the food. Eilis talked of a holiday opportunity and wished she had her own sister to leave the kids with. A comic piece came on the radio and Eilis laughed and said, "That is the way my relations down the country speak." Aisling did not complain when Eilis left the room to get her clothes. Aisling had been just awake before I came in and was slowly coming to. As she woke up she made more sounds but still not many. Aisling enjoyed hanging over Eilis's knee for her nappy change and getting her clothes on. She had her nose wiped continuously. Eilis said that the nurse had said that if she's not sick she should get the "jabs" (vaccinations) and so Eilis said, "That's what we'll do."

She said today, also, that the mark on Aisling's hairline might not go and someone had said that laser treatment works better the younger the child. Aisling jumped at one stage and I thought she was going to fall, she was enjoying being jostled about. I said that Aisling hadn't cried when Eilis had left the room and she said she's happier now—a lot to do with her teeth. Eilis said, "Aisling, will we brush your hair?", and Aisling beamed at her. Eilis put a band on her hair and said, "Everyone has to know that we have a girl in this house." Aisling crawled off quickly and made one attempt to swipe off the band and then found "Duplo" to play with.

She pulled herself up to stand at a sharply edged corner kitchen unit, balancing well on glossy magazines. After a while the lot started to shift and Eilis moved her with her toys to stand at a chair. She said that Aisling wants to stand all the time. Earlier, Eilis had taken a piece of meat from Aisling which was left from dinner the previous day, and which she had found on the floor and was about to eat. Now Eilis started to sweep the floor and Aisling started to crawl into the dirt. Eilis was warding Aisling off with her foot and trying to brush up the dirt at the same time. Eilis laughed, "So much for sterilising bottles. She could have been sucking on the meat that was lying on the floor since yesterday." Eilis said to Aisling, "Here, empty the washing machine for me," and she opened it and got the basket for her.

Aisling went exploring and then came back to the washing machine and started to pull out the clothes as Eilis had demonstrated. Eilis said at the sink, "I'm getting back to myself—I was thinking there that so is Aisling." Eilis said, "Aisling, we'll have to put on your coat." She picked her up and holding her facing me, started to put on the siren-suit and then said, "Oh, you want your bottle, here it is," and started to feed her. As I was leaving, Eilis said, "She's waving to you, Margaret," and I turned around and waved, and Aisling twice gave me a little wave.

Visit thirty-six

9 am on 12 November

42 weeks and 6 days (10 months)

Eilis opened the door and I went into the kitchen. Aisling was eating a peeled apple. She smiled and jumped up and down and put her hand out with an "aaaahhhh" for me to take it. Aisling was completely outgoing today, with her old confidence back, and her nose was not runny. Eilis mentioned again that Aisling does not really like her breakfast as she made it up for her. Eilis did a quick sweep around the kitchen. Aisling started to follow her and dropped her apple. She went to the radiator and Eilis said, "Don't touch," and, "Those are your trousers, Aisling." Aisling was looking back at me and smiling. She got very dirty when the kitchen dirt was swept up and she came back from her travels around the kitchen to put herself right on top of it. Eilis put the piece of apple in the bin. Eilis strapped Aisling into her chair, wiping loose pieces of dirt off her hands and feet with her hands. Aisling started to shout and make fake grimaces and Eilis said, "Oh, that is really pathetic, Aisling," and then, "You are putting it on, Aisling." Aisling stopped and started until breakfast was ready and Eilis was surprised that she was hungry and *did* like it.

After eating, Aisling was dancing and trying to clap hands to the music and Eilis said, "She's really good for a bit of craic." Aisling was very funny and showing her bottom-teeth-grimace which is very comical. Eilis said that she is real show-off and a joker with the boys now. When sweeping the floor, Eilis said, "I wonder if Mac makes a mess like this at work." She told me about swapping days at work to be at home with the children on their day off. Aisling was eating a biscuit. She was shouting and singing a lot today.

Eilis went out of the room and Aisling did not cry. She had let Aisling out of her chair after breakfast and Aisling now followed her into the sitting-room. Aisling was able to get up onto the sofa and she played piano for a while. Eilis said, "Where's Daddy?" as it is Mac who usually plays the piano. Aisling was in a very good mood today. When I left the two were on the couch going through the umpteenth bag of clothes to sort them and find washing, etc.

Visit thirty-seven

9 am on 19 November

42 weeks and 6 days

Aisling waved, "Hello," today and I waved back. Refurbishment was going on in the house and there was a discarded door and door-surrounds in the garden and bits of wood and dust everywhere. Eilis said, "I've a man in doing some work. I've learned more about wood and building this week." Aisling was at the end of the hall on the floor beaming again today.

Eilis put Aisling into her chair and when Aisling moaned and turned down her lip, Eilis said that she had already spent time in there today. Eilis made up her breakfast. She stared at the digestive biscuits when Eilis brought over coffee to us and Eilis gave her one and she enjoyed it. She enjoyed using the tips of her fingers to break off and feed bits to herself. Aisling put up a bit of a struggle today when getting her face cleaned with baby wipes. Aisling was put into her high chair again after having her clothes changed and moaned as Eilis went to answer the telephone although she could see her mother through the doorway.

Aisling showed me her teeth scrunching up her face. Then she jiggled and sang while having her breakfast and listening to her "Smurf" tape but didn't finish the breakfast. Aisling leaned over to give me a kiss after she'd given Eilis one. She cried a little when Eilis went out to make a phone call about the building work. Aisling played around the builder when he came and allowed herself to be lifted by him at one point. She played for ages with three magnets on the fridge, trying to get one off and trying to put it on again. She played for some time until she lost one of them under the fridge and Eilis had to answer the telephone. She kneels and stands very competently now. At one point, Aisling got her fingers stuck in the door of the press and was squeezing the door closed on them. I ran over, grabbed her, brought her to Eilis on the phone in the hall, and she thought about crying but didn't. Eilis said, "She's as tough as nails."

When she came back from the call, Eilis said that Donal wants a real Dalmatian puppy with a red lead and there is no Santa if he does not get one. Eilis said that the man doing the building was very funny and had a great sense of humour. Aisling was crawling happily all over the floor with building dust all over her. She was at the door in the hall and she allowed the man to lift her without protest and to bring her to the kitchen when he needed to get past her.

Aisling was in great form for this visit and Eilis commented on this and that she puts on a show for the boys and is so lucky to have so many people looking out for her.

Visit thirty-eight

9 am on 25 November

43 weeks and 6 days (10 months and 1 week)

I thought that there was no one home when I called at the door. It transpired that Eilis was there but her car was not in the drive. Aisling was in the hallway in her pyjamas when Eilis opened the door and gave me a big grin. There were signs of renovation work everywhere. Eilis showed me where the plasterwork had had to be replaced in lots of places and said that the job was more expensive than had first been thought. Eilis picked up Aisling while she told me this and all this time Aisling was trying to catch my eye and smiling at me and seemed in great humour.

Eilis put Aisling down in the kitchen and she wobbled around the presses before coming over and attempting to climb up Eilis's leg at the sink. Eilis put her in her highchair and strapped her in for her breakfast. Being nearer to me now, Aisling gave me a few mischievous grins. She now has a repertoire of special faces that she does for entertainment. She also showed me her bottom teeth a few times before starting her low-energy moan of discontent.

When out of her chair, Aisling was playing with a hurl that Eilis had given her and Eilis told me how she had almost cancelled my visit because she had been supposed to work and then she had realised, late the previous evening, that Mac had travelled abroad with her car keys—and so she could go nowhere and could not get away from the builders. She was going to walk Donal to a party that afternoon. She was quite annoyed with Mac and said that he, "Is always doing things like this," continuing that if he minds Aisling, he loses her stuff, and she gave a long list of his own possessions that he has lost.

Aisling was doing her low energy moan "aaahh", which sounded unconvincing and phony but somewhat irritating, and which, after some time, is therefore effective. Eilis, smiling, said, "Here's your breakfast […] tinker […] maggot." At different times, Aisling grinned widely and at other times moaned. A different male building worker came in and said "hello" to Aisling; she smiled and then started to cry, making strange sounds. He went out and Aisling resumed her low energy "off and on" crying. Eilis said "That's a joke, Aisling, cry properly or shut up."

Aisling's eyes were glued to the plate of biscuits that Eilis put on the table along with the coffee just as she started to feed Aisling her breakfast. Aisling leaned up out of her chair to get a closer look and Eilis said, "Have one, Margaret, if you dare." Aisling was hungry and ate all her breakfast after an unenthusiastic start. Eilis was surprised. Eilis gave Aisling a digestive biscuit which she bit pieces off. Aisling also played with a plastic toy burger which had a moving figure in the centre and made a noise. Eilis started it a few times for Aisling and then came back from time to time to start it again when it had stopped.

Aisling also bit at it and seemed to be getting some relief for her teeth from it. She sang to herself and said "bababa" and "daaa" and "mam". The phone rang and I was surprised that Aisling cried when Eilis went to answer it in the hall. It was Mac's mother asking about the keys and Eilis explained that she had checked the house but she was sure that Mac had them. She finished the call because Aisling was shouting out to her. Eilis came back in and said, "You're getting fed up in there." She took Aisling out and I changed chairs to see her while Eilis changed and dressed her. Aisling did not object at all and enjoyed the different perspectives. Eilis gave her lots of hugs and slapped her belly when she was naked. She pointed out the nipples that had not flattened. Aisling's nose was running again today and she had a bad episode of coughing as she finished her breakfast.

Eilis played tickling with Aisling and then dressed her, telling her to push her arms in and which Aisling seemed to do. Eilis said, "Are you going to brush your hair, Aisling?" and gave her a brush. Then she showed me how Aisling can stand alone whilst waving the hairbrush with Eilis ready to grab her from behind if she toppled. I had to stand in order to be able to see, then, as Eilis was folding clothes on the table and Aisling went around the table. She played with a pile of drawing paper for a while. Aisling now has four bottom teeth, two incisors, and the teeth in the middle are starting to grow down.

Visit thirty-nine

9 am on 3 December

44 weeks and 6 days (10.5 months)

Eilis smiled as she opened the door and Aisling was behind her in the hall with a puzzled look. Eilis and I walked into the kitchen and Aisling wanted to stay out in the hall, maybe trying out the new floor. Eilis said that she wants her own space and that she is fed up of all these builders on top of her. Eilis had to pick up Aisling and carry her into the kitchen and close the door. As she did, I was getting the "I'm not sure that I am happy she is here" look from her. Eilis felt her feet and spoke to her and then put her into her chair. She said "I will get you your breakfast" and commented on the offer on the cereal pack as Aisling tried out a few moans with a pained expression. Then she started her "special smiles" and began to get very frustrated and tried to kneel up although she was strapped in, just as her breakfast came. Aisling eyed up the digestive biscuits again today, which was after Eilis had fed her, but when she was given one, she chewed off a few crumbs and picked at the edge with her finger-nail. She tried to lick the food from around her mouth whilst having breakfast and then instead squashed her face onto the tray of the chair and proceeded to suck off the cereal. Then Eilis stopped her when she started to suck the screw and Eilis cleaned the slot saying, "There's food in there for six months." She cleaned up Aisling's face and nose and Aisling had a look that said something like, "I rule the universe."

Eilis let Aisling out of her chair eventually and Aisling got hold of the small digital toy and spent a long while holding onto Eilis with one hand and banging the toy off the floor then watching her own and its reflection in the glass French doors as she whacked it off the glass. She talked to it and shouted at it at the same time and then Eilis said, "Donal will kill you if you break it, Aisling." Eventually, as Aisling was getting more gleeful, and the hits were getting harder, she took it off her and gave her a hairbrush instead.

Eilis cleared the plates from the breakfast table and I asked her if she was going away for Christmas, meaning to plan the visits which we would miss, and we made our arrangements. Eilis spoke of the previous Christmas when all of her family but herself knew of her sister's separation. She cries every Christmas Day but it is great for the kids and she was pleased when she read Pol's essay about last year. She spoke of her sister's ex-husband and his inability to make up his mind about what he wants.

Eilis spoke of the possibility that Aisling might have inverted nipples and a woman who was able to express breast milk for her three children despite having inverted nipples. She spoke about the virtue in making the best of things and of a friend whose child was born with a physical disability after the parents had waited eight years for a child.

Aisling was down at Eilis's side and I had my head almost under the table to see her. Eilis lifted Aisling and stoked her hair and said that she might not have a dress on but she would certainly have a bow today and that she, Eilis, could not wait to put something in Aisling's hair, she is so cute. Aisling showed her teeth and they both began to admire Aisling's body and make smacking noises on her legs. Aisling began a game of "peep" with me under the table and stood alone shaking a cardigan and talking to it.

Visit forty

9 am on 10 December

45 weeks and 6 days (11 months)

I explained that I could stay only half an hour today as I arrived and commented that the decorations were lovely. Aisling gave me half a smile from her chair. She was waiting for her breakfast. Eilis sat down to feed Aisling her breakfast although Aisling was unenthusiastic and yet she still ate most of it.

Eilis told me that Aisling had walked the length of the sitting-room twice at the weekend but not since. She said that the day before, Aisling had had her second vaccination. I asked if Aisling had had a reaction and Eilis said that she had not. Eilis also told me that Aisling can go up and down stairs now and is very careful. Eilis commented that her nose is not runny anymore and that she still has her cough and will for a while. Aisling jiggled in her chair when the signature tune of a daily radio programme came on the radio.

Eilis said that Aisling loves music and that she is so undemanding when compared to her brothers and that she had been in the highchair since she got up. Eilis answered the telephone and Aisling wailed, made a face, and eventually emitted one cry. She calmed herself, listened, and then the same again. Then two tears fell and I smiled and said, "No, no," and she decided not to cry. Eilis came in and asked if Aisling had been crying and I said that she had been going to and changed her mind. Eilis took her out of the chair, gave her a cuddle, and sat opposite me and started to dress Aisling.

I waved at Aisling and she smiled but she did not wave back. Her hair is getting longer and can be brushed back now and changes Aisling's appearance and the blotch on her hairline seems much faded.

Visit forty-one

9 am on 17 December

46 weeks and 1 day

Aisling was in the middle of breakfast when I arrived. She seemed in good form though her nose was running and she still had her cough. The kitchen was in serious disarray and there were two beautifully decorated Christmas cakes on the table, as though all efforts had focused on making them. Eilis commented that "It's mad"—but she didn't really seem to mind. She brought in a singing Christmas tree that Mac had bought and Aisling jiggled and grinned to it. Then Eilis put on a music tape for Aisling who danced when she eventually got out of her highchair. The hour went by with Aisling singing and dancing to the singing Christmas tree, the radio, and her tapes as though she was putting on her own Christmas concert.

Visit forty-two

9 am on 7 January

48 weeks and 1 day (11 months and 3.5 weeks)

Eilis answered the door smiling. Aisling was not pleased to see me as she sat in her highchair, watching me. I moved to a chair further away, as I thought that it was too close for her comfort. Aisling was turning the pages in her block book. Eilis talked about how she and Aisling were sick and Aisling had been sick with an ear infection over the Christmas and had "made strange" when the two of them were abroad visiting Eilis's family. Eilis is off work this week with a sore throat for which she had taken antibiotics. Aisling's hair had grown and was very even, as though it had been trimmed, and she eventually gave me a smile.

I asked how Aisling's walking was going and Eilis said that she's walking all the time now and managing in her shoes. Aisling was getting impatient and was trying to take off her pyjamas. Eilis stood in front of Aisling to feed her and when she gagged she took the food away immediately and threw it in the bin, saying, "It will turn your stomach."

Eilis made coffee and brought out Christmas cake. The radio was on and she said, "Look, she loves the music," and then, "That was Merry Christmas—she's trying to speak." Eilis says, "Yes," and then, "Say 'no.'" Aisling pointed to a picture of a teddy bear in her book when her mother asked her where he was. She shakes her head when she picks things off the floor as if telling herself, "Dirty! Don't put it in your mouth."

Aisling smiled broadly when Eilis took her on to her lap—it did seem to be what she had wanted all along. Aisling loved getting her clothes off but protested by crying briefly when having her clothes put on. now points to things, walks competently, and picks things up from standing. She uses her fingers dexterously and she knows not to put things in her mouth. She now wears a clip in her hair which her mother says that she loves. Aisling took the hairbrush from her mother and brushed her mother's hair.

Visit forty-three

9 am on 14 January

362 days

When Eilis let me in, I walked after her and when Aisling saw me, she gave me a fleeting smile in greeting which was very much happier than the suspicious look of the previous week. Aisling was fidgeting in her highchair, putting her feet against the side bar as if to hoist herself out and then changing her mind. She played with a book and tossed it overboard and looked at me as if to say, "I'm bored." She has a slight grimace, as if deciding whether or not she will cry, bored and wanting to get out of the chair and impatiently waiting for breakfast. She repeatedly put her foot against the side of the chair as if to lever herself out, giving up and trying again. Her facial expression was one of dissatisfaction. She tried to get her soother a few times and was frustrated in this also as her chair strap was over the soother strap, so that the strap didn't reach her mouth. Aisling's nose is running again. She went through the pages on her book and turned back and forth a few times before looking plaintively at me whilst knocking it overboard. After a few moans, Eilis put a spoon on the table and that also was rejected.

Eilis told me Aisling's news: that she had slept well the night before but not for the two nights before that. Aisling has three back teeth coming through on one side. There is a ridge on the other side which is likely also to be a tooth. When they are down, that will be fourteen teeth in total that she has. Eilis attributes Aisling's clinginess, running nose, ear infection, and the fact that she is not eating or sleeping properly, to these teeth.

Aisling had started to whine and Eilis said, "It's coming." Eilis brought over coffee and gave Aisling one spoon of her breakfast and went back for her own coffee and biscuits. Eilis asked me if I thought that Aisling was thin. I said that I thought that she'd grown tall. Aisling did not eat all of her breakfast and Eilis said that she was surprised that she had eaten as much as she had. Eilis said that Aisling gags if she has had enough and then I saw her do this.

Eilis was at the sink and Aisling started to stand up and get out of her chair. I said it to Eilis and she came quickly and started to put Aisling's straps on properly, remarking that it had been Mac who had put on the straps. Then she doubted herself and thought that it was Pol and then, "Anyway, I suppose the straps are difficult, they're twenty-three years old."

I said that Aisling will be a one-year-old soon. Eilis said, "Yes," and, "It's been a wonderful year, I'm not running to buy shoes for her like I was for Pol. It's lovely to have a baby with you; you're never short of a cuddle or someone to need you." Eilis said that Aisling has another vaccination, then her developmental check coming up, and she wishes that it was the other way around. Aisling follows instructions. Eilis told her to shake her head, show her "teddy", show her "hair", and make a "phone call". She also put her rattle between her teeth so as to have both hands free to wave them. Aisling spent time opening and closing things and she went about and gathered her clothes into a pile.

Visit forty-four

9 am on 24 January

1 year and 10 days

Eilis telephoned to say that she was working on the day of the visit and so we rescheduled. When I got there that morning, Eilis made Aisling's breakfast quickly. Aisling had a badly congested nose. Her hair is thick and wavy now. She had a beaker cup and was following Eilis around and leaning on her leg, bent over from the waist. Eilis commented on the congested nose and said that she has "snail trails" all over her clothes from it. She said that Aisling's nose is congested because she has teeth coming. She said that they are going out to buy Aisling's shoes tomorrow. Aisling pulled bags out of the cupboard. Eilis gave her a container without its lid and she went about the kitchen looking at things with the container under her arm, looking at things and putting her hand into the container. Aisling watched Eilis as she tidied things off the counter tops into the cupboards. Aisling seemed to be imitating Eilis's activity and she did this until close to the end of the visit, when Eilis brought her over to the kitchen table and sat down on a chair there with Aisling's clothes to dress her, just as I was leaving.

Visit forty-five

9 am on 28 January

1 year and 15 days

Aisling was in her chair and waiting for her breakfast, which Eilis made up quickly for her. Eilis told me that she had something to show me and she had Aisling out of her chair and dressed quite quickly today. There was a great air of celebration of Aisling's milestone of her first birthday and getting proper outdoor shoes, and when I told Eilis that we had about fourteen weeks to go until the end of the observation she started to reminisce. Aisling followed Eilis around and to hang out of Eilis's legs but she also spent minutes very much doing her own thing, and she was very interested in the contents of the cupboards, opening them up one after another and spending some minutes on one before she moved on to the next. Taking things out to inspect them carefully and when she tired of them, putting them back or throwing them on the floor.

When Eilis brushed Aisling's hair, it really looked lovely and then Aisling spent some time showing off all the things she can do—her "tricks" as Eilis called them. Aisling's nose is still congested but does not seem to bother her. Aisling followed Eilis into the sitting room and she found her shoe (which was what was being celebrated), when Eilis asked her to. Eilis found one and Aisling found the other.

Eilis put on Aisling's shoes and she walked, conscious of her shoes, in the kitchen. She walked confidently and bent to pick things up and carried things in both hands. Eilis commented that Mac had suggested that Aisling was showing a real interest in clothes and that Eilis had assured him that Aisling was simply imitating her.

Visit fourty-six

7.30 pm on 13 February

13 months

I'd had to cancel the previous visit and when I telephoned, Eilis asked me to call in the evening the next week as she had to work. When Mac opened the door, there was a lot of action in the hall. Eilis was in the hall. Aisling came out of the playroom, passing me with her too-long trousers rolled down and one leg of her trousers over her shoe. She was listening to the different noises of her two feet on the wooden floor. I followed Eilis into the sitting-room and Aisling came in, taking note of my arrival and going past to be near to Eilis. Aisling took the armrest cover off the sofa, shook it around, and then put it back on the arm. Eilis said, "Yes, that's where that goes." And to me—"she knows." Eilis talked about how busy things are and mentioned a radio programme.

Pol was going overnight to the scouts and everyone went into the hall to wave him off. Aisling stood at the door waving out at him and he came back and hugged her about three times. He was going when Eilis called him back and got a kiss and a hug from him. She told him she probably wouldn't sleep, with him out of the house, whilst hugging him and then winked at me. Eilis called out to Mac that he had not got his lights on. Aisling stayed where she was for all this and waved Pol off and closed the door when Eilis told her to. Back in the sitting-room,

Eilis said that she was just in and about to have a coffee and offered me one.

I followed Aisling, who followed Eilis out to the kitchen. Aisling looked up at Eilis and made the moaning "Aaa" sound that she makes when waiting for her breakfast and pulled at Eilis's skirt. She wanted to be picked up and Eilis offered her a biscuit which she refused. Then we went back into the sitting room and Eilis said, "She's been great," mouthing something about her being easier than the others—Gavan and Donal were still in the house. Aisling had found a toy coke bottle, which is in fact a microphone, and was singing "Aaa" into it. Eilis commented that she was able to use it correctly. Aisling went over to Eilis now on the sofa and climbed up. She started to test the sound on different surfaces, including her hand, but went back to the sound it made on the sofa as her preference.

Aisling got a biscuit from Eilis. She stood beside Eilis and broke it in bits and put it on the sofa and took a taste of one piece, put that down, and then another. Eilis told me all Aisling's tricks: she says "Baby" for her doll and "Po-po" for Pol. Eilis asked her repeatedly to say it as she wandered around the furniture and she did and then turned to me and grinned and repeated it. Aisling got up on Eilis and tried to sit on her lap but had to settle for sitting beside her because of the hot coffee. Donal came down the stairs calling Mac and Eilis said that he was gone out with Pol and Donal said the computer was still on. Donal sat up on the side of the couch and Eilis told him to get off because I was watching Aisling and they had a discussion about how tall and advanced Aisling is compared to other children.

Aisling was standing on the sofa exploring behind the cushions and found a bit of paper that Eilis told her to put in the bin but Aisling didn't oblige. Gavan came in, Eilis asked for a hug because she hadn't seen them all day and she commented on how lovely they are and that when she's been away she sees how lovely they are and she could just eat them. The three of them sat on the floor. Aisling fed the boys pieces of her biscuit. There was a discussion about what the boys might eat or drink and what was in the fridge, and the two boys settled on drinks.

When they came back, Aisling was very excited and Donal started to give her some of his by squeezing it out. Aisling seemed to have the technique of sucking and I moved over to see but Aisling looked at me and stopped and I moved back but could see, when she resumed, that she was sucking through the straw. She went over and back between the two boys and everyone was watching her and marveling at her doing this. Eilis said that Aisling now has sixteen teeth. The boys told Eilis jokes and Aisling laughed with the others and Eilis said she has a sense of humour. Aisling went out in the hall and took Donal's spelling notebook out of his bag and came back into the sitting room. He grabbed it saying, "Don't even think about it, Aisling." She was not in the least bit perturbed.

Aisling started to run from one sofa to the other, bouncing herself off the sides. Eilis commented that she does that with the pouffe and she ran to the pouffe, on hearing the word, I thought. I heard the story of the party for Aisling and the doll, and Eilis sent Donal out for the doll and Aisling grabbed it from him at the door and pulled at the opening of the dolls suit at the back and put it to her nose. Donal laughed and said, "She's checking the nappy." Aisling gave the doll-baby a hug when asked to and put it down and Eilis rocked it and said, "Ah, the baby," while Aisling watched. Aisling got back up on the sofa and reached over the top and found a nappy which Eilis put on the doll but the game was over and Aisling was now exploring the sofa. She tried to climb up the back and slid right down on her back as the cushion gave way. Everyone laughed and then Eilis tickled her and she continued laughing. The homemade Valintine's cards were shown and Eilis and Donal inspected Pol's—"From one of your three sons, Pol, in case you've forgotten." Donal showed me his card and then his sticker book. When Gavan came over, Aisling stood right beside me, and put her index finger over to touch the book once or twice.

Mac came back and threw in sweets to the assembled company in the room and proceeded to the kitchen. There were two packs and the boys gave Aisling one sweet each. Blue dribbles came down Aisling's chin and went onto the already chocolate-stained white cardigan. Donal asked would the stains come out and Eilis said she had a special soap bar for it.

Donal started to do headstands and Eilis told him to be careful. Then there was a game of chasing around the back of the sofa and Eilis shouted to Gavan to stop and said, "Now, I told you," when Aisling banged her head under the piano stool. Eilis took Aisling on her knee to console her as she yelled and when Donal came back from the kitchen blowing a recorder, she stopped but Eilis was telling him that that was dangerous too. Aisling was on Eilis's knee in the sitting-room and Gavan was in the kitchen complaining to Mac about Eilis blaming him as I left.

Visit forty-seven

3 pm on 25 February

13 months and 12 days

When I arrived at the house, Pol was outside on the doorstep making weapons, and there were stones and knives and sticks on the ground and he shouted in, "Mam, Margaret is here," through the letterbox. Gavan jumped up on the inside of the front door to open it. Gavan, Donal, and Aisling were in the kitchen making pictures with blo-pens and stencils and there was artwork of this kind already hanging on the wall. Aisling was sitting up with a pen in hand. I noted that she had very pink cheeks and Eilis commented that she was just awake so she should be in good form and, "Oh, you've never seen her just after her sleep." The two boys were engaged in comparing their drawings and they seemed to be vying a little. Aisling was trying to do what they were doing and they helped her.

Eilis was talking of incidences of meningitis when Gavan said, "Mine's full of spit," and she had to attend to this. Donal and Gavan were vying for things. Aisling was stretching up past her head with two of the pens and looking at me as she did this. She gave me a wide berth when the doorbell went and she wanted to see who was there. It was Pol and he brought in his weapons for Eilis to admire. Eilis made coffee and gave Aisling a chocolate biscuit because she had already had her dinner whereas the others were going to eat when they went for a fast-food tea.

Gavan was not happy with this and was standing on a box in order to look in all the cupboards. Aisling got up on it behind him and there was a high level of activity. Then Aisling went over to the table and Eilis was preventing her from getting right up to stand on the table while Donal and Pol came into the kitchen chasing each other with weapons. Eilis shouted at them to stop and when a kick came close to my face she got annoyed. Gavan ran off with the stone from the top of Gavan's weapon and they chased each other around the table. Aisling enjoyed it and when they were wrestling under the table, Aisling went right in and crawled over them while Eilis was telling them to watch out for her. Aisling seemed serene and fearless today. At one stage she was pulling Gavan off Eilis's knee, so she could climb onto it. And when Donal was putting brown pen on Gavan's bottom, and tempers were becoming frayed and mixed with mostly high spirits, Aisling crawled over the two fighting boys as they wrestled and took the disputed object away to investigate it herself.

Eilis was relaxed throughout and Aisling was calm under her mother's watchful eye and showed great self-possession. Aisling got herself right in beside the boys under the table when they were wrestling each other. There was a very high level of activity and noise today but at the same time as things were also contained and very child-centred.

Visit forty-eight

9 am on 4 March

13 months and 19 days

Aisling was wearing her overcoat when I arrived. She came right up and tapped me on the back. She had wanted to go outside, Eilis told me, but she had been sick during the week with a cough and a temperature but fortunately had managed this time without an antibiotic. Aisling and Eilis played at finding Aisling's navel—"Where is your belly button?"— while Aisling was being dressed and there was lots of laughter.

Eilis figured that the separations she had when she had been at work and Aisling was teething were contributing to Aisling's upset. And Aisling had had constipation and was waking a lot during the night. Aisling came right up and went around and tapped me on the back. But then she did not know what to do. Eilis cuddled Aisling with her bottle for a time to allow Aisling to go to sleep if she wanted to. But Aisling pushed Eilis's hand away from the bottle, got off her knee, and brought her nappy to the bin. Aisling says "this" for things that she wants and points now. She was able to hunker down and balance and sway to music whilst eating crisps. Aisling began to roll about on the floor. My approach interrupted her in her daydreaming while lying on the floor and went for hugs of reassurance from Eilis and she spent some time getting hugs and tapping Eilis on the shoulder and saying, "Mama." She followed Eilis around as she swept the floor. Eilis said that she is not used to silence and put on music that included the songs "Carrickfergus" and "Ride On". She reports that Aisling is sleeping in the bed with her while Mac is away and is sleeping better. Eilis said that she got a fright the other day when Donal came around and let himself in at the back of the house. She had to tell Aisling to mind her fingers twice as she played with the kitchen drawers and then she opened the pot drawer for Aisling to play with it. Today, Gavan was rough with Aisling whilst Donal made a box for her hair ties. Aisling is to get her vaccinations and hearing test next week.

Visit forty-nine

7 pm on 11 March

13 months and 26 days ·

I came at an unusual time this week. Eilis had forgotten that I was coming. Aisling was wearing a navy dress with a tartan trim and was smiling and following Eilis around the kitchen. She tried to sweep the kitchen floor with the garden brush and she really has the correct sweeping action. Eilis gave Aisling two baking tins which she put over her head and then slammed them down with glee. Donal asked for a cereal bar. Aisling went quickly over and shouted at him to show that she wanted some and he opened it and gave it to her and then went over to Eilis and they watched Aisling as she tried to eat it, making faces. Aisling was smiling today. Gavan came in and got a yogurt and Aisling wanted some and he gave her some but she wanted to feed herself. Eilis put her in her chair to feed herself but the straps could not be found. She stood up and had to be taken out and Eilis kept her on her knee. Eilis said that Aisling was not eating well and has slimmed down and that she wants to feed herself. Eilis let Aisling try to feed herself with the back of a spoon. The scene that followed was extremely messy and extremely enjoyable for Aisling. There was yogurt everywhere and Aisling looked like she was in pleasure heaven. After she had tried to feed herself with the back of the spoon, Aisling tried to pour the yogurt into her mouth and then she put it on both hands and she sucked the yogurt off her hands with a big grin. Mac came in from leaving Pol at Scouts and made himself tea and sat beside Eilis for a while. Aisling went to get up on his lap and she said "up-up" twice. In that time Aisling went over to Mac and he passed her back to Eilis and went out. Aisling was sliding in the yogurt when Eilis went to get her pyjamas and baby wipes to clean her. Aisling was running up and down the kitchen and trying to engage Gavan as I was leaving.

Visit fifty

9 am on 20 March

14 months and 5 days

Aisling had her coat on when I arrived. And she followed Eilis around and wanted to be picked up. Eilis said that Aisling was off her food as she made her breakfast. She lifted Aisling into her chair but was laughing as, although she was saying, "Sit," and trying to get Aisling to bend her legs, she could not get her in. When Aisling was sitting, Eilis fed Aisling her breakfast. Eilis uses two spoons now, one for herself and one for Aisling. But Aisling was not interested in her breakfast and didn't like it. Eilis took Aisling out of her chair and she followed Eilis around and Aisling "swept" the floor as Eilis picked things up. Aisling followed Eilis around the kitchen picking things up. She stood with two hands on the freezer looking into the fridge in a way that seemed to be copying what she had seen the boys doing. Aisling pointed to things on the work surface that interested her saying "that". Eilis took her on her lap and they looked at her picture book together and Aisling pointed and said, "That." She dressed her and Aisling pulled over the baby wipes predicting correctly that she was going to have her face and hands cleaned. Eilis reported that Aisling, who still has a runny nose, had failed the "rice rattle" but not the "bricks" item at her hearing test. Aisling went about the floor with the dustpan and brush and she put things in the bin.

Visit fifty-one

8.45 am on 25 March

14 months and 10 days

Mac opened the door to me and he and the boys were standing in the hall about to leave. Donal and Eilis had a few cross words about Gavan's party in the afternoon. Aisling was there too. She was wearing a hooded jacket of Eilis's on her head. Donal asked me had the system for bins changed where I lived too. Aisling waved goodbye to her Dad and the boys with Eilis standing behind her watching that she wouldn't fall out the door. Aisling seemed to cry after Pol particularly. It stopped as soon as they were gone and the door was closed and Aisling was no longer upset.

Donal had said that there was a dirty nappy and Eilis started to change it as soon as we went into the kitchen with Aisling over her knee as always. Aisling is so long now her head hangs over but she still seems to enjoy the different perspective this activity offers as she stays quite still. Aisling was then dressed and started to pull at the baby wipes predicting that they were to be used next. Eilis commented that she knew to get the wipes. It was difficult to get Aisling to bend her legs to be put into her chair. She said, "Sit," at the time that Eilis was trying to get her to sit. Eilis gave Aisling breakfast with a spoon each but Aisling was not interested and the breakfast went in the bin.

Eilis let her down out of her chair saying, "Where are your shoes?" Aisling looked over to her padded slippers and Eilis said, "Oh, you want those ones," and Aisling smiled. Aisling was doing a lot of pointing and saying "dith", "eth", and "dath", and I wondered if she had said "dress". Aisling was in good form and gave me big grins from time to time. Only once did she look at me as if to say, "Get away." She wandered about the kitchen sweeping a bit and then she went into the vegetable cupboard. She got out an onion and took the dry peel off before discarding it. She took a red pepper and presented it to Eilis who was at the sink all this time. Eilis took it and looked at it and gave it back. Then Aisling came and presented it to me and ran off and came back almost immediately and repeated this.

Eilis went out into the hall and Aisling, bravely, did not follow immediately but leaned into the furthest corner looking around, eyeballing me and eating the half pear that Eilis had given her. Aisling then ran and followed Eilis out into the hall and went into the downstairs toilet and stood under her coat, pointing up and crying until Eilis put it on her. Aisling held her arms out appropriately, having walked off with the coat half on, on two occasions.

Eilis told me that Aisling had had her last "jab" (vaccination) the day before and was very upset. She also checked that she had told me about Aisling failing her hearing test and that Aisling has an appointment with Sister Lydia (audiologist) and that Eilis is getting Gavan tested also as he speaks very loudly. Eilis was trying to get Aisling to follow commands. When the phone rang Aisling followed Eilis to the hall, went to explore and look out the window of the front room but got shy and stood with Eilis's legs in front of her, "hiding" beside the front door. Back in the kitchen Aisling went to the back door looked out and said, "Out"—she wanted to go out all the time I was there.

Eilis asked had Aisling eaten all the pear and I said she had. She called Aisling and asked her did she want another piece and Aisling nodded. Eilis cut the core out while Aisling watched and took the pear when offered it. She opened the press doors in front of the dishwasher. She peeped down the side and up into the handle. Then she hugged it, feeling the vibration. Eilis repeatedly asked Aisling to put the clothes into the basket on the floor and Aisling put in some, leaving some. There was pretend play with Aisling smacking and kissing the basket and when her feelings became intense, Aisling then looked to be lifted by Eilis. She got a hug and Eilis asked her would she do her hair. Aisling touched her head on hearing the word. During the visit, Eilis said that of course she thinks Aisling is a genius. Eilis told how Donal saw Aisling's two-year-old cousin hit Aisling. She got very upset and Donal was very annoyed. She told me that Aisling is allowed out in the back garden sometimes. "She's mad to be off," Eilis said.

Eilis said that Aisling was to have her developmental check and she wished that she had had the vaccination after it, as she might be upset at her developmental check. Eilis said she still has beautiful hands and she's not overweight—"I certainly won't be ticked off about that with you." Eilis was rubbing Aisling's hands and generally admiring her and then she started to look at the book with her—"Where's teddy?", "Where's bottle?", "Where's ball?", etc. Aisling looked at the book and then Eilis and then back to the book. She thumped the book but did not point this time as Eilis had wanted. She touched her hair when asked, "Where's your lovely hair?"

Eilis took Aisling out of the chair to dress her. Aisling was relieved to get out. She walked around the kitchen very competently. Eilis took Aisling on her lap facing me to dress her. Aisling put up her arms when asked. She loves getting her clothes off—she smacks her belly and grins. Eilis cleaned her face and hands with baby wipes.

Aisling had a spoon in one hand and a rattle in the other. When it came to getting her clothes on, there was a struggle to get her to surrender them for the few seconds. She started to put the spoon through the circle of the rattle—Eilis commented. Aisling's game started with the wipes box: Eilis had to open it so that Aisling could close it and give it a "good bang". At one stage, she put the rattle between her teeth to do this, then she pulled Eilis's hand open and got her to hold the rattle.

When Eilis put her down, she went and had the same game with the detergent compartment on the dishwasher door. When she started to get up on the door, Eilis closed it and Aisling went to the other side of the kitchen, starting to empty a press of nappies and plastic bags.

The phone rang and Eilis said, "She's going to follow me, Margaret." Aisling followed Eilis at speed and fell on the wooden floor when she had reached Eilis. Aisling saw me looking at her and her return look was one of, "This is your fault—where's my mammy?"

Eilis came back from the phone with Aisling in her arms to check something on her calender and I said it was time for me to go and was this time next week okay? Aisling was more relaxed in her mum's arms. I said that I hoped she enjoys her birthday and left as Eilis was resuming her conversation.

Visit fifty-two

3 April

14 months and 18 days

Eilis answered the door. Aisling was in highchair smiling and eating toast and sticking her fingers into it. She slid squares of toast off the edge and Eilis picked them up. Donal called to Eilis for his toast from upstairs as I began to arrange finishing dates with her. He was home, sick. Eilis was subdued, sad, or angry at the idea of the observation finishing or a bit of all three. Eilis gave Donal his toast and made coffee. She hugged Aisling and this was the first time that I saw Aisling wriggle so much when she was getting dressed. The hugs were more for Eilis than for Aisling, I felt on this occasion. Aisling found Donal and played fetch with him with lots of vocalising.

Eilis told me about Aisling's hearing test—her hearing was down in her left ear and she was slow to turn for the maracas on the right also. Sr. Lydia has asked if she said "mam" or "dada" and Eilis said that she had but then stopped. She had only been able to test her right ear as Aisling was upset because of having her vaccination so recently. Eilis gave Aisling softened cornflakes and a spoon. Aisling repeatedly used the back of her spoon and sucked it but used her index finger and thumb of the other hand to pop cornflakes into her mouth. Eilis saw that

Aisling was making slow progress and she sat and fed her and Aisling ate enthusiastically for the first time in weeks. Aisling is on ordinary milk now and taking it well. Eilis spoke of going on her Easter holiday with her brother whose child has physical difficulties. She said that she will enjoy it and that it is the only way that she can see her family.

When the kitchen door was opened Aisling ran into Donal who was on the couch with his duvet watching TV and looking at a book. Aisling sat and watched Donal and I while Eilis put a top knot into her hair. When she had her hair done, Aisling came over and gave me a toy man that Eilis had given to her. Then she ran over and sat beside Donal on the couch and he gave her a ball. Eilis went over and checked Aisling's hair and then went out of the sitting-room. She got off the couch and Donal asked her did she want to play "fetch" and he threw the ball for her and she brought it back to him repeatedly. There was lots of point- ing, vocalising, saying "this" and "that" to Donal at this time. When Eilis went on the telephone, Aisling ran between the kitchen, the hall, and the sitting-room.

Visit fifty-three

10 am on 6 April

14 months and 21 days

I rearranged this visit as the family were going to be away for some time for their Easter holiday. Mac let me in and Aisling was in the hallway in her pyjamas. She had a red face and a runny nose and when she saw me she ran back in to Eilis in the kitchen who was looking for Calpol for her as she was ill. Eilis said, "Hello," and that she had been up since dawn with Aisling. Eilis was going around the kitchen tidying and Aisling was following and leaning against her leg wanting to be lifted. Eilis did lift Aisling and carried her around with her while she searched for the Calpol. Eilis put Aisling in her chair and gave her the medicine and tried her with breakfast, which she refused. The breakfast went in the bin. Eilis took Aisling on her knee and gave her a cuddle and Mac asked Eilis if she knew where his jumper was and later where his savings book might be.

Aisling seemed quiet but not distressed. Eilis gave Aisling the last of her bottle, which she took willingly. Eilis made coffee and brought them over while carrying Aisling. Aisling pushed her blocks, which Eilis gave her, around on the table in a low energy way. She enjoyed Eilis's cuddle. Eilis talked and Aisling got a little lively towards the end of the visit when her cheeks seemed to fade and the medicine seemed to begin to take effect. She took a little walk into the sitting room, watching to see if I'd follow. Eilis was beginning to dress her as I left. The boys were upstairs on the computer.

Visit fifty-four

14 April

14 months and 29 days

Pol answered the door with Aisling in his arms. He said that his mother was getting dressed and that she would be down in a minute. Aisling looked thinner than when I had last seen her. She was pale, in her pyjamas, and her hair was stuck back on her head with food and snot and her nose was running but she seemed contented and secure with Pol. He brought Aisling into the sitting-room, saying that she could watch the TV. Aisling would not let Pol put her down on his first attempt and he stayed with her for a few seconds until it was okay. He said, "I'll put on the TV, Aisling," and she let go. Pol seemed very grown up and gentle. He said that Aisling had a dirty nappy and added that his mum was awake but his aunt was asleep.

Eilis came down and said, "Hello. It's cold and it's lovely to stay in bed," and she asked if I had had a good Easter. Eilis set about Aisling's nappy. Aisling had had to go to a doctor in Wicklow as her left ear was infected. Eilis's sister, also called Aisling, came in and gave Eilis her post. Aisling imitated Eilis with the post. Aisling went over for hugs from Pol. He made a face and asked Eilis to take her as she was smelly and that she smelled of poo. Eilis protested that she wasn't and that she had just cleaned her and that her bottom was the cleanest part of her.

Eilis's sister asked about my visits while Eilis took a phone call. Aisling ran into the hall a few times to check if I would follow. Eilis told Donal that Aisling was saying hello to him when he ignored her approach and Gavan was just coming in as I left. I said that I was not sure if the next visit was the last or second last, and Eilis said that it was the last.

Last visit

2 pm on 24 April

1 year, 3 months and 5 days

I got to the visit a few minutes late. Eilis answered the door with Aisling standing in the hall behind her. They were both dressed up more than usual and Aisling had already had her breakfast. Aisling was wearing a navy floral cord pinafore with white blouse, white jacket, lacey ankle socks, and a topknot in her hair. She had a tea towel around her neck until just before the end of the visit. Aisling smiled at me and ran back into the kitchen. Later Eilis told me that she had asked Aisling a few minutes before I'd arrived, "Where's Margaret?", and Aisling had run to the door.

Eilis went into the kitchen and over to the sink. She said, "Find a seat there, Margaret, there's one with no cereal on it." Aisling circled the floor, seeing what she could see on the worktops. She took down a piece of brown bread, the heel, and a knife and Eilis said, "Do you want bread? I'll get you a nice piece," and took both things from Aisling who changed her mind and shook her head. Aisling shadowed her mother and at one stage hid behind her mother's dress, peeping out at me. I said, "Peep," at one stage which was an intrusion and she hid for a good while.

Eilis offered me fruit soda bread, which I had with coffee which Eilis brought over for both of us. Aisling pretended that she was stuck getting up on a chair over beside her mother at the sink and now again on the one beside her at the table. Eventually she sat up and Eilis gave her a piece of the soda bread and she licked the butter a few times and made a face at me. She went on to Eilis's knee briefly before getting down and walking around the kitchen. Aisling came back to the table closer to me and I tilted my plate towards her to take the remaining piece of bread which she did.

Eilis went over and pulled a block of cheese off the work surface. Eilis went over and cut a piece off for her, saying that she has some reach now and that she likes salty things. Eilis said that Aisling is obsessed with the fridge and stands looking in and will look for ham slices if she knows they're in there.

Eilis cleared the table and was wiping it and the highchair down. Aisling went over to the press and took out a duster, spray cleanser, and what looked like polish but was fly killer. I said, "Oh, she's going to do cleaning," and Eilis said, "Oh, Mammy has those but she never uses them—she's useless, Baby." I had to tell Eilis that Aisling was sucking the nozzle of the fly killer. Eilis took the stuff off Aisling who went for more cheese, which Eilis gave her. She spat it out on the floor and Eilis said, "Oh, you tink," and wiped it up with some toilet paper that was lying on the floor. Aisling looked at me and ran to the kitchen door as if to run out but the door was closed and she ran and hid behind Eilis at the worktop again.

Aisling stood looking into the fridge as Eilis put things into it. (It's on top of the freezer so she can't reach in or see in very well.) Eilis said that she was in a friend's big old house and that Aisling had run off and found the fridge which was a long way off. She said that Aisling was clever to do this and different to the boys who used stick close to her.

Eilis gave Aisling candy sticks which she tried to open with her fingers and teeth. Eilis went to answer the phone and Aisling ran after her and Eilis opened the pack. Aisling could not get one out and Eilis did it for her. When Eilis hung up she told Aisling to give me one and she tried. Eilis took one out and said, "Give it to Margaret," and Aisling did. Eilis took one also and there was some reminiscing about these "sugar cigarettes". Aisling opened her mouth to show me that she had a whole one broken up in there. Eilis went into the kitchen to check something for Mac and went to telephone him back.

Back in the kitchen, I said, "I've something for Aisling in the car," and went to get it. Eilis said she'd watch that Aisling didn't follow. Aisling started to wave and I said, "I've confused you," to her. Eilis said, "You can take it out and show it to her," from the sink and then she came over and said, "She loves dresses," as Aisling traced her finger on the designs. I gave Eilis flowers and she showed them to Aisling who touched them and made a face. Eilis said, "It's so sad that it's over," and took out a knife and started to chop the ends off the flowers. I felt a strain and Aisling was standing at the patio doors looking out as if she wanted to go out. Eilis looked strained and then was smiling when she came back with a vase with withered flowers that had been in it since Mother's Day.

Eilis brought out the photos of Aisling and there was talk of the different stages that the baby's hair had gone through. Eilis said that they had taken very little video of Aisling and have loads of the boys and that the video recorder is broken and will have to be fixed for the holidays. (Aisling was forgotten for some minutes.) Aisling went after Eilis when she was returning the pictures to the room and I commented that Gavan was six when I saw the cards and Eilis said, "It's a month and I can't bear to take down the cards as they brighten the room," and she showed me the Mother's Day cards from Donal and Gavan— "When I'm naughty and you want to shout at me, relax instead, and have a cup of tea." Inside there was a real tea bag in a picture of a tea-pot. Eilis showed it to Aisling who was pulling at her and then she put it back on the mirror.

Back in the kitchen I sat and watched as Eilis let Aisling carry a pack of toilet rolls. She looked comical—like she was a grown woman. Eilis put them in the press and Aisling opened the press and started to pull out her nappies.

I thanked Eilis for allowing the intrusion of the visits and said that I was lucky that I wouldn't have any concerns about Aisling as I knew that that was not always the experience of others completing baby observation exercises. Eilis asked how work was going and talked about helping a boy with his biology and about her reflexology course. She mentioned a child in her son's class who has really no one to care for him and she talked about a discussion on the radio about "Our Lady of Fatima", seeing children burning in hell. Someone had telephoned in and said that many children are in hell on earth.

Eilis lifted up Aisling and walked to the hall with me when I said it was time to go, saying how the time had flown and it was so sad it was finished. She told Aisling to give me a kiss and Aisling leaned over and I kissed her cheek and Eilis leaned forward and we hugged and I stepped outside. I asked her to thank Mac and the boys for me and said I'd phone on the nineteenth of September about a list of milestones that I'd taken on Aisling. Aisling was pottering in the garden as I drove away with Eilis waving. I was glad to finish for Aisling's sake, as it was she who felt and acknowledged the intrusion of my visits. I enjoyed these visits and missed them, whilst also feeling relief that they were over.

CHAPTER SIX

Baby observation report

This report is divided into the following sections:

Observation background
The baby
The observer role
Getting to know aelf through feeding
The ego integrates
Beginning, middle, and end sample visits

Observation background

This observation took the form of weekly fifty-minute visits. My first visit was to the hospital when the baby was one day old. All other visits took place at home. The baby's mother was present for all visits. My last visit was when the baby was fifteen months old.

There was one visit before the birth. This was my first time to meet the parents, Eilis and Mac, in person and my first contact with the baby's father of any kind. He took the opportunity to "check me out" and to be sure that he was happy with what was being proposed. I was left with a feeling of the father as a person who was interested and protecting his family from a distance. He was agreeable to the observation though not going to take an active part. This couple struck me as united, happy, child-centred, and looking forward with excitement to this baby. I left this visit with the arrangement that Father would call me after the birth but in fact Mother called, from the hospital and left a message on my answering machine on the evening of the birth.

Baby is the fourth in this family and the first and only girl. She is also born four years after the third child. The boys, at the beginning of the observation, are: Pol, eight years; Donal, six years; and Gavan, four years. Parents did not know the sex of the baby during the pregnancy. Mother told me on the visit which took place before the birth that they had been very busy with the boys as babies as they were all babies together and she was looking forward to having time to "enjoy" this baby, although she felt more tired during this pregnancy and attributed this to increased age. She was looking forward to one set of nappies, etc.

Mother is of Irish parents living abroad and Father is Irish. The couple met abroad. When I started this observation it was clear that Mother would often be on her own and that she missed the company of her own family, especially at this time, and particularly her four sisters. I continued to feel throughout the observation, that my visits were in some way this mother's attempt to compensate for the distance between her and her siblings. The maternal grandmother had died some years previously and the maternal grandfather less than two years before. This baby was the first to be born since the grandfather had died.

The baby's father's parents were living in Ireland and there was quite a lot of contact, much of it initiated by the baby's mother and seeming to compensate a little in relation to her loss of her own parents. Mother kept close contact with her family. One of her brothers, and all but one of her sisters, were in the house on a visit with their own families on separate observation sessions.

This household presented mainly as child-centred, relaxed, and happy throughout the period of the observation. Father was active in the childrearing and, when there, a "hands-on dad", hearing spellings, putting the children to bed, making the dinner, feeding the baby or changing her nappy. Father's job took him abroad quite often, mostly for days at a time, but on other occasions for weeks.

Baby's arrival was met with a tremendous welcome and great excitement, particularly because she was a girl. This was particularly significant to Mother who misses the company of her sisters. Mother, a professional person, works at one and a half hours' commute from home and was not sure, when she was expecting her baby, about her return to work. She did in fact return, as a jobsharer, which was the arrangement she had before the birth, but now doing full days which reduced the commuting and left her with full days at home.

The woman at the end of the street, who had been looking after the boys after school, took the baby also when Mother returned to work when Baby was eight months old.

There was a great sense of relaxation and fun in this household for the most part. There was a great sense of fun between Mother and the boys when they were there. All three boys showed great care for their sister and enjoyed the novelty in the early days of her being a girl.

The baby

There seem to have been very little outward signs of celebration at the baby's arrival and yet there was huge quiet joy with Mother and then with the other family members. There was a theme of great joy, happiness, and pride about her arrival. She was considered perfect and in the early days everything had to be perfect for her.

Baby's arrival was unusually welcome and brought an instant "love affair", first with the mother and then with the other members of the family, which has now translated into a very special and secure place for her in the family and a quiet and self-assured sense of herself. Over her first summer there has been a sense of great happiness, relaxation and pride in this house: first Mother's, and then Father's, and then the boys' pride in and enjoyment of their sister. Her arrival seems to have added something extra and special to their sense of themselves. It has been from this very firm base that Baby has been broadening her horizons.

Baby now is a very happy little girl who enjoys her family and is enjoyed by them. She lives in a very child-centred house where she holds a unique position. She is, for the most part, hungry for experience, mobility, and broadening her horizon. She is sure of herself, having had calm, attentive, and "good enough" parenting. She is now able to wait to be picked up, to get her breakfast, or to go out. She has a good sense of herself and has good perseverance when solving the little problems which she encounters in her exploration of, or interaction with, the environment. Now that she can tolerate separations, she is impatiently hungry for adventure and broader horizons.

The observer role: a neutral, benign, or malign container?

With a fourth baby, part of Mother's agreeing to participate in the observation was that this baby being observed would make it special. This was agreed towards the end of the pregnancy and before the sex of the baby was known. The fact that the baby was born a girl and four years after the last child was more than enough reason, as things transpired, for her to have a unique and special status immediately. The decision to become involved was made in pregnancy by the baby's mother.

From the outset the observation was something that I feel Mother wanted for herself as well as for Baby. Living, as she does, in a different country from her siblings, I feel that she particularly wanted someone to witness and share the experience of this baby in a way that her siblings, and especially her sisters might have, were they living in the same country, rather than in the only way they could with telephone contact and very occasional visits.

For Mother also, it became apparent that she invests a lot in her role as a mother. She has a very child-centred home, takes an active interest in her own and other people's children, and has limited her hours spent in her professional career in a way which she feels allows her to maximise her input to her family. There was something in my psychological contract with Mother that made my observation a reassurance or confirmation that she was "getting it right".

The contract to be involved with the observation was made primarily with the mother and she negotiated it with her partner and children. As this mother was there for all the visits and father for very few, it was probably as well that the major part of the agreement was with her.

Because of what seemed at times to be this mother's feelings, which she reported, of separation, loss, or sometimes loneliness, the maintenance of the role of observer rather than that of friend or confidante was, at times, hard to keep. For my part, I feel that this is an impressive, competent, and warm woman and someone with whom, in other circumstances, I could perhaps have a rewarding friendship.

On one or two occasions, because he is not usually there, I felt that the baby's father found my observation visits as mildly intrusive on his time, space, and his attention to his family. There were also occasions when he was there that this was not the case. On no occasion except for the one on which I gave notice of the approach of the end of the observation, did I feel stress or strain around my visits. On that occasion the strain was due to the mother's disappointment, and my own, that the end was in view.

On a visit early in the observation, the second son offered me the baby to hold and was quite offended, on the baby's behalf, when I declined the offer. I got help from the mother on this occasion, reassuring him that I could only look at the baby. In the early days the visits were a little resented by the youngest son because of the focus of attention on the baby from me and by the extra attention given to the baby by the mother. This soon passed and the boys became very used to achieving a balance between facilitating me to see the baby on the one hand and ignoring me on the other.

The baby herself, in the early months, seemed oblivious to my observing her. The first time she looked at me was an achievement of head control and focusing. Then there was what seemed to be recognition that mine was a face like the other faces in the room and the feeling that the roles were reversed and I was being scrutinised as someone new and different from herself—as though the "not me" object was recognised. Then there was the feeling that she recognised and remembered having seen me before.

At the seven-month stage she was fretful, sometimes frightened, and certainly wary. The welcoming smile was often, at this stage, replaced by a worried frown. Around this time also, the baby, on a few occasions, showed, by becoming distracted or inhibited, that I had come physically too close and she waited until I moved back to resume her activity. As the weeks went by, and certainly from about nine months onwards, an acceptable and automatic distance between us was established from which baby was happy to be observed.

When baby became mobile, she played with the boundaries of this space on occasions. She approached me from the back and patted my back on one occasion. Later she brought objects to me to hold which she would retrieve soon afterwards. When she first went in her walker at seven months she would approach me soon after my arrival and touch my clothes. Later she became too wary to do this for a time.

Later again, when walking independently, she would run from room to room on occasions to see if I would follow her. Sometimes this was a welcome game and at other times it was clear that it was an intrusion, from her expression or from her attempts to hide behind Mother, etc.

On one occasion she was lying on the floor beside Mother in a particularly deep state of reverie, humming to herself and rolling around on the floor whilst gazing at the presses. She seemed absorbed in a daydream of which Mother was a part. My moving positions to see her face on this occasion seemed to have been experienced as profoundly intrusive and disturbing.

As time went on and the baby became more mobile and independent, my observation felt progressively more intrusive and restricting to her. Baby would often look out into the garden as though wishing to be out there or try to get out the kitchen door. Certainly any time the opportunity to get to another part of the house presented itself, she was off. Mother sometimes had to reclaim Baby from the stairs during my last visits and she would look to have her coat put on which, in turn, signaled going out.

In retrospect, I am enormously grateful to all members of this family for allowing the intrusion that my visits must have been from time to time for all members of the family as well as for Baby but which only Baby showed. These visits formed a pleasant part of my week and until the time when the end was near I looked forward to them.

However, the observer role was one which, on occasions, was hard to maintain. At the beginning it was easier. As time went on, the unease that the baby felt with my arrival, the intrusion into her transitional space or reverie on occasions, and the restriction that it represented in the latter stage, made it uncomfortable on occasions. Sometimes, when Mother left the room, for example, it was difficult to gauge how much of Baby's distress was at Mother's absence or my presence.

From the point of view of what I represented for this mother, it was, at times, hard to keep observer status. It was obvious that I was going to be given information about this baby as though I was preserving mother's experience of her baby for her—giving it some extra validity or reality. Mother talked quite a lot on each visit, sharing what life was like with the baby for her and what life was like for the boys, her husband, and the whole family.

There was comfort in the fact that, because of my observer position, this mother was aware that, for the most part, I would not respond to what she said and she was happy to continue talking knowing that. Much of what she told me was of Baby's day-to-day progress and was, I feel sure, the kind of thing that she would have reported to her parents had they been alive or to her sisters if more contact were possible.

Towards the end of the observation, I increasingly found it hard to keep the majority of my attention on Baby. I feel that this is to do with the baby's welcoming of the fact that babyhood was finishing and that greater independence and freedom was on its way. By contrast, the mother's feelings were much more ambivalent and associated with feelings of loss and anxiety at Baby growing up and of herself and her family moving on to another stage and away from one which she had been enjoying so much.

As the observation finished, I felt that the baby would feel relieved and released. Mother however had some slight feelings of anger and loss which manifested in her questioning the finishing time (which was, in fact, early) at first and then reminiscing and saying how sad it was that "it" was over. I feel that the "it" was the babyhood of this, likely to be her last, baby as much as "it" was the observation. At this time the observer status did not seem enough for the baby's mother and I felt as though I was withholding something.

This mother realised consciously, to some extent, that she was reluctant to leave this stage and that there was something more general about her sense of loss. This was poignantly represented for me in the last visit when I gave Mother flowers to say "Thanks". She went to put the flowers in a vase on the mantelpiece in the sitting room, where she still had the Mother's Day cards that the children had made her and the cards for Gavan's birthday, even though both events were over by months. She had an awareness of this and laughed at herself for keeping things long after the event had passed. She was accepting and gracious about the ending, even if unhappy about it. The transient nature of the observation and her baby's babyhood seemed to present this woman with some fear or anxiety.

I feel that my observation had a function of holding (Winnicott) or containing and at times detoxifying (Bion) this mother's anxiety about the baby on some occasions; for example, when, at five months, there was the worry that the baby might have cystic fibrosis, or, at four months, when I visited during an acute attack of colic, then this woman, who was there alone, seemed to become calmer, even though there was no significant reduction in the baby's distress during the first half of my visit.

There was also an amount of identification between myself and her in both of us being mothers and living in the same part of the city. At the end, I also felt an ambivalence about my role of observer from this woman who may have felt somewhat torn between the wish to make more of her career and to be present in every way as much as possible to her children—in her role as a mother she was generously allowing me to profit for my career.

For the baby, the mechanisms that seemed to be most at play were those of projection and introjection. When the internal object was experienced as good, then the visit was welcomed as though there was something good that could come from outside. When there was a lot of persecutory anxiety for the baby, for example, especially at the nine month stage, which was a time of teething, pain, and more frequent separations from her mother, I seemed to represent the outside into which the badness had been projected. My coming in seemed to represent to the baby the possibility of having to re-introject the bad cut-off and projected persecutory objects. This is how I account for the significant variation in the baby's greeting of me from week to week. One week I got a huge smile and a "come hither" welcome and the next week it was replaced with the frowning wariness that told me to keep my distance.

During the observation, the baby's growing sense of self was mirrored by her increasing sensitivity about being observed. The observation's reciprocal nature and her capacity to determine what happened, for example, when she came behind me, handed things into my hand, hid, or stopped doing something until I retreated.

Getting to know self through feeding

The beginning: the nursing couple

Mother told me, during her pregnancy, that she had breastfed the others as babies. She also reported that she felt particularly tired during this pregnancy, so there was a doubt as to whether she would do so on this occasion. On my first visit to the baby, when she was one day old, in hospital, this mother's response to her baby fidgeting on her shoulder was to try to feed her, and when she was having difficulty getting the baby to latch on, she was able to say that this had been the pattern earlier in the day and to persist in a calm manner. I feel that this characterised the notable feature of this mother's handling of the baby and her capacity to hold her baby's anxiety. There was a surety in the way she handled her baby which, I feel, contributed to the establishment of the baby's confidence in relation to the world and boundaries of the "self".

At one point the baby let go but continued to suck loudly not knowing the "me" or the "not me" of the breast. On this occasion on the right breast, baby was angry at the breast and screamed loudly at it when she became detached. Her mother's capacity to remain calm at this point, and to attribute the difficulty to the fact that the baby was drowsy, meant that the mother was able to continue calmly to hold or detoxify what seemed a very frustrating and persecutory experience for the baby. On this occasion also, when the mother changed her baby to the other breast, the baby latched on easily, fed, and fell asleep as though she had split off the persecutory anxiety and left it in the other breast.

At home

On the third visit, at two and a half weeks, the baby was reported to be "as good as gold" and to be feeding and sleeping well. She fed during the visit and her mother reported that the baby was clever and knew to pull away from the breast when the milk was coming too fast. The baby gazed at her mother in concentration while feeding and also between feeding spurts.

It seemed for the next month or so that this kind of time taken over feeding was part of the process of Mother and Baby becoming part of each other's "transitional space" (Winnicott) or of "reverie" (Bion). At one stage Mother told me of her friend's difficulty with an older child, when she was besotted with a new baby. She said that she did not want to make the older children suffer because of her preoccupation with her baby. It seemed to me, at the time, that this mother was referring to being immersed in the "primary maternal preoccupation" and enjoying it, while to a degree acknowledging how difficult that is for the displaced siblings.

When the baby squirmed and put her head to one side at one stage, her mother took this as a sign that she was hungry and said "You're hungry, you poor pet", and spoke to her until she settled into feeding. I am reminded in this of Daniel Stern's notion of the mother constructing the baby's reality. In this case, this mother's attribution of cause of distress or rage in the baby was to real and external factors, which allowed her to feel safe that she could solve the baby's problem, and she responded with calmness and empathy. At one stage, on this visit, the baby let go of the breast and continued to smack her lips loudly. Her mother said that the baby knew she was doing this now. There was a faster flow from the right breast and her mother said that the baby just licks that breast and knows that she does not have to suck. The baby hummed while feeding and, when she pulled away, panted, and her mother said "I know, it's hard work". This mother took the baby's wriggling and "messing", that is, her latching on and letting go repeatedly, to mean that she had wind or a "poo" and took pleasure in "knowing" the baby well enough to predict correctly.

On the fourth visit, when this mother reported that she thought her baby had an upset tummy because she herself had eaten broccoli, it seemed particularly evident that the boundary between the two individuals of mother and baby was not yet definitely drawn.

At times, the baby brought her hands towards her mouth and opened her mouth as though dreaming of the breast and, at other times, her mother was correct in taking the baby's head-bobbing as a sign that she was hungry and she latched on and fed immediately. The baby had a preferred breast, which was well-established by this stage. Her mother said "Don't do that, you'll pay for it later" when the baby started to gulp and said that she was worried that this baby would have colic, as her oldest brother had. Then the baby pulled away and Mother felt her tummy and said "It's all hard", as her baby wriggled and she rubbed her back until the baby burped a moment later. There seemed to be wonderful attunement between this mother and baby and the fact that this mother accurately predicted that the baby had wind and dealt with it so calmly and quickly meant that an otherwise unpleasant experience of their time together was avoided. It seems significant also that this episode would have contributed to this baby's growing awareness of herself and her "insides", that is, the space between her head and toes, between where the food goes in and comes out.

Halfway through the fifth visit, this mother picked up her baby who was screaming loudly and put her to the less preferred breast—the left—where baby continued to wriggle and "mess". Because they had to go out directly after the visit finished, she then put the baby to the preferred breast where she immediately latched on and fed intently.

On this occasion, the mother was asking her baby to withstand the frustration of having to take the preferred breast after she had first fed from the non-preferred one. The first small step into the process of disillusionment had been taken.

On visit six, when the baby was forty days old, the mother was tired and the baby was sleeping after a three-and-a-half-hour screaming episode of colic. Mother looked tired and upset and Baby, who was now sleeping, sobbed in her sleep occasionally. There was a striking similarity in the mood of both. There were two things apparent in this visit: the shared identity and attunement between the two; the increase in Baby's ability to tolerate frustration and Mother's willingness to let her—as they were going out after this visit, Mother said "You'll have to wait" to Baby when she woke and cried loudly as Mother gathered the baby's belongings necessary for the trip. Baby fed calmly and intently, having had her nappy changed, as we left.

Ruthless love—the mother allows herself to be used

On the seventh visit, when Baby was more than forty days old, she was feeding fast and with very strong sucks when I arrived. Mother said that Baby had become a very strong feeder and could empty the breast in seven minutes. Then Baby was gripped by pain and seemed to be sticking her tongue in and out as though to expel something bad. Baby shook her head and yelled at the right and preferred breast, as though experiencing the breast as the bad and persecutory object, having projected the internally experienced pain into it.

The baby's concept of "me" and "not me" seems to be well-developed for this to happen. After letting go a few times and yelling and groaning at the breast, Baby latched on and fed strongly. Mother reported that Baby was getting "assertive" and had scratched her a few times. The baby's experience of the fact that her needs and those of her mother are different and not identical, must serve to establish, a little more distinctly, their distinct and separate identities.

Baby's ambivalent and sometimes persecutory, as well as at times gratifying, feelings about the breast were in evidence again on the eighth visit, when Baby fed strongly at first and then pulled away from the breast and first played with it and then seemed to get annoyed with it, making an "inging" sound. When a spiral of winding, seeing if she wanted to feed, and winding again, ensued, Mother stayed calm and treated this as pain—"It's great when you get to know them. She's going to do something. I can feel her tummy", she said. Baby got a bit sick, did a noisy "poo" and then smiled at Mother. Mother had withstood the destructive and greedy attack. After being changed and fed, Baby went on the right breast and fed seriously. Mother's feeling that she knew what was happening seemed to contain or detoxify the baby's anxiety and in return Baby gave Mother the pleasure of being correct and giving comfort.

A temporary leak

On visit nine, at seven weeks and two days, the situation was very different. I arrived and Baby was still crying but somewhat calmer, after another more serious colic episode which lasted four and a half hours, during which Baby screamed all of the time. Mother was exhausted and shaken and a much more "porous container" than I had witnessed on the previous visit. On this visit, more than on any previous visit, I felt that my presence helped Mother to contain her anxiety and helped her, in turn, to contain Baby's anxiety. I felt this, as I have said, because Mother began to behave as though the episode was over as soon as I arrived even though there was no perceptible let-up in the baby's crying until halfway through the visit. Baby burped and was a little sick and had started to feed as I left.

The depressive position

On visit ten, aged about eight weeks, Baby had had two ounces of milk from a bottle. She was congested and unable to breath through her nose. She slept with her soother in her mouth. She fed strongly but pulled away frequently, as she could not breathe and feed well at the same time. At one point when she pulled away, the breast milk was coming so strongly that she must have felt this, the usually preferred breast, to be overwhelming whilst she had nasal congestion. The non-preferred breast, with its weaker flow, might have been, in this instance, more gratifying and less persecutory than the right and usually preferred breast. The good part object (the preferred right breast) might have been more integrated with the split-off bad part object (the non-preferred left breast), and the baby's relation to the whole object, emerging.

On the twelfth visit, Baby was sick and Mother's concern and sadness about this was emphasised in the fact that there was no feed during this visit and Mother got medicine into her baby mechanically by means of a pipette. There was a sense of separation or loss in the listlessness of both. The period of primary preoccupation is over—the object of the pipette, for example, coming between the baby and the mother.

At fourteen weeks five days, on the fifteenth visit, Baby has now had experience of the breast in her mouth, she has put her fingers in her mouth and Mother discourages that by giving her the soother. She has had experience of various things in her mouth and her experience is expanding. She has been having one lot of fruit and rice since visit thirteen and now is having two lots per day. Baby's appearance has changed since the introduction of solids and she now has folds of skin on her neck. Mother is enjoying the experience of feeding; she says that she loves when Baby puts her hands around her breast when she is feeding and hopes to continue until after they return from their summer holiday. Baby feeds a little, stops, and looks at Mother as if to say "Hello"—as one whole object to another—before resuming. Mother talks to Baby from time to time and fondles her hair, wondering what colour it will eventually remain. The experience of feeding seems to provide the opportunity for a shared reality or playing, as well as inner and outer reality, to emerge. The space that exists between the two is becoming enriched and growing, as well as allowing the opportunity for their individual and separate selves to be recognised.

On visit sixteen, at fifteen weeks five days, Baby again seemed to be playing at the breast. She would latch on, feed, let go, look at Mother, lean back and grin, then start again. Eventually Mother got Baby to feed seriously for three minutes at the non-preferred breast and Mother says "Well, I've won the battle this time". Mother seems to be increasing the demand on Baby in this visit; she is also encouraging her to breastfeed more than she has been inclined to since two bottles were introduced.

A real and ordinary person—the kitchen will do

The introduction of solids seems to mark a new departure and visit seventeen takes place in the kitchen, as do most subsequent visits. Mother is standing at the table feeding Baby rice. Baby is in her carry chair on the table. She is happy to be fed and gives grins to people who come into the kitchen. Baby is putting her hands into her mouth after the food and sticking her tongue in and out. Mother attributes this action to teething. Mother feels that Baby is comfort-feeding at night for the feeds she is missing during the day since the introduction of the solids. Mother may feel somewhat disregarded, that Baby has replaced the breast and, to that extent her, with a new object—food. On visit eighteen, Baby is gripped with a pain for the whole visit and Mother walks her up and down and tries to comfort her with breastfeeding. She eventually settles to this as I am leaving—this feels like a temporary regression before moving to the next developmental stage.

For the next few visits it seems that Baby now can get comfort from food and still revert to the breast to get food or comfort. The baby seems to have integrated the two into her world. On visit twenty-two, at twenty-one weeks and five days, Baby ate her breakfast very quickly and then stuck her fist into her mouth. Mother reported that she had been under pressure the previous day and had not had enough breast-milk. She also reported that Baby, who was sticking out her tongue and drooling during this visit, had an oddly shaped mouth, which was an unusual thing for her to say as Baby is usually referred to in positive superlatives. It was as though the pressure that Mother was feeling, the lack of breastmilk, and the oddly shaped mouth were in some way linked as Mother and Baby shared a special, though in this case perse-cutory, space together. This was the last visit before a six-week break from visits and also a time when, because of the introduction of sol-ids and teething, Baby seemed to be de-cathected from the breast and Mother and Baby seemed unsure of their position with regard to each other. During this visit Mother made many positive comments to me about Baby, for example, that she was still besotted with her, as though reassuring herself that the break, or the introduction of solids, would not ruin something which was precious to her.

A break and a change

On visit twenty-three, after the break of six weeks, when Baby is six months old, she is offered the breast and is not interested. Baby is also "too busy" on visits twenty-four and twenty-five. She is on four bottles per day now and is given chocolate during my visit and lemonade from a cup when she starts to choke. Her world seems to have expanded, as well as her mobility and subsequent capacity to explore it, and Mother and her self seem to have developed their contact so that now it is Mother's closeness and presence that Baby seeks—the whole object—rather than the breast. Baby ate her breakfast whilst sitting on Mother's knee. On visit twenty-nine, she had refused the bottle on the previous night while with a babysitter and now ate breakfast, given by Mother, so fast that Mother said she would have a pain. After this, Baby fell asleep with the comfort of a cuddle.

On visit thirty, at thirty-six weeks and three days, that is, eight months, Baby was putting her hand and toy into her mouth after her food. She sucked so hard that part of her face disappeared into her mouth with each suck. She choked on a piece of biscuit but that did not deter her in any way from continuing to eat. It was as though her food appetite and her appetite to ingest experience were in parallel. On visit thirty-one, the nurse had weighed Baby during the week as part of her development check, and Mother was proud to announce that Baby was just a little over what she should be—"Not big busters as the others had been". Again, this was like a public acknowledgement for this mother that what had been a "private affair" between herself and her baby had been executed correctly.

Doing

On visit thirty-two, Baby was biting pieces of apple hard and making faces because of the tartness—it was like a visual display of ambivalence; enjoying the destructive attack on the persecutory anxiety of teething by biting on the one hand, whilst at the same time being repulsed by the taste. At this time also, Baby starts to be given pieces of food, for example, the slices of apple which she can finger feed and carry about with her whilst she is engaging in the exploration and introjection of information from her environment. The growth of the self is also represented at this stage by the baby's capacity to retrieve food which has been lost or previously discarded—she can now feed herself and is encouraged in these attempts by being given her own spoon whilst Mother feeds her. It is as though the pieces of food that she is given to carry about on occasions are like transitional phenomena which she uses in her ebbing and flowing journey from dependence to independence—a secure base from which to enjoy her adventures.

Revisiting base—depressive anxiety

On visit thirty-four, Baby is reported to be clingy. She is off her food and fiddles in a despondent way with the top of her bottle, letting it spill but not drinking from it. By the end of the visit she is sitting on Mother's knee happily sucking her soother and relating to Mother as whole object.

On visit thirty-nine, Baby refuses her breakfast but her eyes light up when the digestive biscuits are produced. Mother notes that Baby gags if she does not want her food and the breakfast is disposed of promptly. By taking the digestive after she has refused the breakfast, it may be that Baby is ambivalent about Mother and trying to reinforce the boundary between the two. During this visit also, Baby forages on the floor and shakes her head when Mother says "No, dirty". Mother says that Baby shakes her head when Mother says "dirty". It is as though the baby is learning that there are two kinds of things—things that belong inside and things that don't. She shares this reality with Mother. By acknowledging that there are two categories, she can distinguish between herself and Mother: the "me" and the "not me"; inside and out; external and inner psychic reality. By the game of the shaking of the head, the potential space between Mother and Baby is used so that they can also have the third area of shared experience.

The beginning of the end of babyhood

The fact that Baby and Mother both had sore throats in the forty-third visit indicates that, in the midst of a lot of establishing of separate identity and greater independence, there still is a relatively great amount of shared reality between them. Baby is sitting bored in the highchair waiting for breakfast, unable to put her soother in her mouth because the string is too short, but tolerating the situation—Mother stating repeatedly that Baby does not like her breakfast anymore. It is as though Mother has done her job well enough that she can be destroyed or rejected in fantasy by the baby so that Baby establishes her sense of self as subject and object as objectively perceived so that real object relatedness is possible.

As if by way of proof, in visit forty-four, Baby fed her brothers pieces of biscuit and allowed herself to be helped drink from a straw. All the children were able to enjoy and share this experience, including Baby.

Being in her body

In visit forty-nine, Baby had a very pleasurable experience feeding herself yogurt with the back of a spoon. The yogurt went everywhere and the baby used her hands then to feed herself and also she just enjoyed squashing the yogurt in her hands and between her fingers. There was a lot of time spent in this visit looking at the food in the fridge with the door open, and playing with the vegetables in the press. It is as though the original instinct of the oral erotogenic zone, that is, to feed, has been broadened to include looking at food, playing with food, and sharing experience of food with others.

The end is near

On visit fifty-three, Mother and Baby had been up since dawn as Baby was sick and running a temperature. Baby took Calpol but refused breakfast and sat in desultory mood on Mother's knee for most of the visit.

Destruction withstood

Visit fifty-five was the final visit. Mother had gotten in fruit soda bread and Baby, who had been walking around the perimeter of the kitchen, came to the centre, as did Mother who had been working in the kitchen, when the coffee and soda bread was produced. It was as though the baby now lived a separate and more independent existence close by, but reverted to a closer proximity and earlier relationship to Mother around the activity of feeding. Feeding and the capacity of food to represent or mark something else, as in this case an ending, seems to have been understood by Baby.

Later in this visit, Mother produced candy-sticks for Baby. The telephone rang then and there was a delay in her getting them as Mother had to open them and Baby had to wait for the short conversation to be over. Mother asked Baby to give me a candy-stick. Baby attempted this but Mother had to do it. Mother reminisced that she had these as a child, inquiring whether I had. I did have and said so. Mother remembered that their name has now been changed from "toy cigarettes" to "candy-sticks".

There seemed to be something significant in the fact that the three of us—Baby, Mother, and I—had one of these each together, whilst Mother acknowledged that although she has had them before they now have a different name and are, at once, the same and new. This, I felt, put a needed link for Mother between past, present, and future so that her difficulties about the ending of the observation—this (her last) baby's babyhood and the identity she had shared with this baby when it was small—were in some way held and made meaningful by this transitional activity or ritual. A "shared space" would continue to exist for mother and daughter, whilst at the same time the Baby's private and independent self has room to emerge.

Ego integration and doing

First half

On my first visit to Baby at home she slept all the time—her eyes not as tightly closed as when first I saw her. She slept propped with cushions on the sofa. Her skin tone changed from white to pink to red and back and her facial expressions changed, with lips puckering, causing Mother to note that she was dreaming. The most striking change was in her physical appearance from week to week. She began to be better able to recognise the breast and distinguish it from her mouth. Her eyes opened and she noted different sensations, such as having her nappy changed, by stilling, or her eyes widening when she had her navel cleaned. Baby started to focus on faces and patterns in the room. She was attracted to light and concentrated on the point where the pattern of the sofa stopped and the light of the room started. Baby at this time also started to move her head and to fan her arms and then her legs. She moved her head to one side as a sign that she was hungry. She distinguished the fast-flowing breast which she need only lick from the one where she needed to work harder to be fed. Baby, in the first weeks, could locate Mother's face when she came in the room and before Mother spoke or touched her. She started to make a humming noise of pleasure when feeding, as well as the distress sounds of hunger or pain.

On visit four, Baby wakes on hearing Mother's voice. She cries but is comforted instantly when lifted. She holds her head up for a few seconds and focuses on my face. Her eyes widen as she moves her gaze from one thing to another. Baby feeds strongly and grimaces in pain but seems to know the relief of a burp is coming when she is held upright.

At thirty-three days, Baby spends the time absorbing things visually. Siting with her hands by her side and head leaning on the side of the carry chair, she focuses on the definite shades and patterns of the fireplace tiles. When she gets hold of my face with her eyes, she can follow it as I move a little. Baby takes a more gradual approach in her call for food. The sounds get progressively louder without getting desperate. Baby "holds out" for the preferred breast and then feeds with intent.

At forty days, Baby and Mother are both tired and despondent following an episode of colic—Baby, asleep, still sighs and sobs occasionally. Her head goes from side to side and her hands go up and down as she sleeps. Later, she enjoys the freedom of nakedness and is temporarily distracted from it by her hunger.

Next visit, Baby seems to be more aware of her legs. Leg movements get faster as pain intensifies. She looks straight at me and seems to smile. Baby tolerates the discomfort of wind and Mother's attempt to clear it. Baby is held by her brother and looks from Mother to me to the print on the sofa. Baby is content and takes things in visually as she is carried facing outwards by Mother as she moves about the room.

Baby's cry is stronger and more persistent now when she has a pain. She has different attitudes to the breast. This varies from the hum of sheer satisfaction and playfulness to torment and rage, when she yells loudly at it or scratches. Baby shows ambivalence at the breast, craving it at the same time as being angry or frustrated by it. Having been gripped by pain, Baby smiles at Mother in recognition of a relieved state, after she gets sick or does a "poo". Baby seems to enjoy the handling, and the different visual perspectives and positions of her body in space that are yielded by the daily routines of washing, dressing, and changing.

At seven weeks and two days, my visit came at the end of a four-hour bout of colic which left Baby exhausted and still in pain. Baby stiffened and contorted her whole body, screaming. Her eyes rolled and she yawned as though only pain kept her awake. In a pain-free second she looked at Mother and smiled, and at me. She relaxed with fists still clenched. Mother's talking to her took her attention and she copied the shapes Mother's mouth made. I wondered if this made the process understandable and available to experience.

On visit ten, Baby can use her head control to look from one picture of her brother to another. She can feed and pull away to draw her breath because her nose is congested. She has a napping routine, so her day has some shape. In the next few weeks, Baby seems to be more aware of looking at people and being looked at. She can get her brothers' attention with a smile as they go by and she can demand a greeting from them. She is better able to turn the trunk of her body and spends time looking at her hands and moving them up to eye level and down again.

During this time, Mother and Baby are somewhat despondent over a few visits. It becomes apparent subsequently that Mother has been worried that what turns out to be bronchialitis was cystic fibrosis.

Baby enjoys being perched on Mother's knees when they are raised so she can see all around the room. She seems to be eager to get going to other places in the room. She is also trying to bring under control those movements necessary for the eating of solids, as she has started on baby rice and excitedly sings, "talks", smiles, sticks her tongue out, and puts her hand in her mouth while Mother tries to feed her. Baby now pulls things and she pulls her bib while feeding.

By the nineteenth visit, Baby can do several things at once. She vocalises, listens to brothers in the kitchen, smiles, kicks, and pulls the blanket covering her as she lies propped on the sofa. On visit twenty, Baby went on the floor for the first time and was able to move from side to side by arching her back. On the next visit she directed herself over to a yellow rabbit up by her right arm.

Baby now is aware of the parts throughout the length of her body. She spends much time playing with her toes or using her finger tips to explore surfaces, for example, the mantelpiece or the necklace that Mother puts in her hand. She looks from one speaker to the other as her two brothers tease each other and she obliges by going to sleep when the preparations for sleep are introduced, that is, when she is put in her carry chair, given her soother, and covered by her blanket. Baby also looks for a cuddle from Mother when she is tired and can go to sleep when she needs.

Second half

Baby moves to the kitchen at this time with the advent of solids and becomes more mobile when she acquires a walker. She uses the tips of her fingers to try to pick up textured flowers on the carpet and can operate the buttons and activities on the walker. At seven months and two days, breastfeeding is finished and Baby scoots around the kitchen in her walker. She approaches me on my arrival and picks at the pattern on my trousers before mouthing it. Another day, it is the buttons on my skirt which she touches and considers mouthing before something at the other end of the kitchen attracts her attention. Baby is constantly active, investigating the whole room and everything in it now that she has newfound freedom and power. Baby shouts until Mother comes and nudges her over the lip on the floor between the wood and the tiles.

Now, when out of the walker, Baby gets about by bottom-shuffling or crawling. Although mobile and hungry for adventure Bay still enjoys the routine of being changed or dressed. New parts are being added to the familiar routine. Baby has her hair brushed and Mother tickles her tummy and slaps her legs and she laughs.

Baby now joins in on Mother's activities—emptying the dishwasher. Baby then tries to go into the dishwasher. She can also make things happen again, for example, pulling Mother's hand back to tap on the wipes box again in a game where they took turns. Baby can create and communicate a new idea from the old, for example, when she turned this game with the wipes into one of "playing the piano", a movement which she has seen Father do. Mother still concedes to enough demands that Baby feels she can make things happen, but by relating and communicating to another rather than by omnipotent fantasy. Baby goes through upset at this time with Mother's return to work. Mother reports that Baby is very clingy when she comes home and looks to be picked up a lot. Baby is able to engage in turn-taking tapping games with her brothers. Baby becomes temporarily wary of me at this time and also cries if Mother leaves the room during my visit. Baby is getting lots of teeth and also has an ear infection at this time.

Mother has to put out the bins during my visit and Baby can comfort herself a little by looking at mother through the glass and tapping at it until she returns.

On visit thirty-five, at forty-two weeks, Baby picks the food off the floor and Mother takes it off her and laughs at the idea that she still sterilises bottles. Baby gives me confident smiles and her teeth and old self-assurance seem to have come through.

Baby looks at me and her Mother as she performs the tricks her brothers have taught her. She sucks in her top lip and waits for the reaction. Mother demonstrates and presents the wash basket and the open washing machine to Baby to take the clothes out of the machine. Baby initially rejects the idea, going to a different part of the room but coming back to it. Baby is able to predict her effect on others and at the same suit and manage herself. It seems the private and public selves to which Winnicott refers are developing in parallel.

In the next few visits it is as though I am associated with the constraints that are put on Baby's movements. She is very happy to show her ever-increasing repertoire of new tricks and she enjoys the routine of dressing and Mother's handling of her which is becoming more elaborate. She also enjoys those activities in which she imitates Mother as part of the ongoing identification process. But Baby is wary of me on my arrival, she sometimes hides from view, and she tries to get out of the room and up the stairs quite often now. Sometimes Baby escapes into an activity and becomes absorbed in it, for example, the arrangement and movement of the fridge magnets. She looks into the fridge, the hall, and the garden, as though she'd like to be there. She is most despondent but patient in her highchair and Mother notes that she likes her breakfast less.

At eleven months, Baby is not happy to see me. She gags her breakfast and is much relieved to get out of the highchair into which she is strapped. Things given to her in the chair are thrown overboard in frustration. Mother says "Are you off galivanting?" as though there is some recognition of Baby's wish to broaden her horizons. But she also says that she is in no hurry to get Baby's first shoes. As if to be clearer in her communications, Baby is wearing her coat in one visit. She has Mother's coat on in the next visit and stands under her coat until it is put on during two other visits at this time. Mother says "She's mad to be off' and that she sometimes goes out in the back garden now. Baby loves going for walks or to collect the boys from school. I seemed to have intruded on a daydream Baby was having during visit forty-eight also.

Baby's capacity for imagining seemed to be increasing at this time. On one occasion she engaged in an activity which involved kissing and then slapping the clothes in the wash basket. Whatever persecutory anxieties were stirred by this activity, Baby ran to Mother for hugs immediately she finished. At this time, Baby engaged in similar activities with a cardigan and on another occasion a small digital toy which she shouted at as she hit it off the window.

On the last two occasions when her brothers were home, Baby was very happy to be near and included in the rough and tumble-type game of wrestling on one occasion and chasing around the furniture on the other. There did seem to be something in Baby's being a girl that made Mother feel the need to protect her more.

CONCLUSION

There is a parallel between the development of self in infancy, in analysis, and between the role of the analyst and the mother's function, and, in Chapters Two to Four, I have followed this parallel through Winnicott's three stages of dependence. Examples from a baby observation and adult analysis are juxtaposed to this end. These also demonstrate the highly applicable and useful nature of Winnicott's psychoanalytic thought in their respective illustration of the good enough and deficient environment.

Before departing on the journey through the stages of dependence, the continuity of thought between Winnicott's thinking and that of his major influences, Freud and Klein, was confirmed in Chapter One and followed by a brief look at the broader trends in child development theory which may have shaped Winnicott's thought.

In the second chapter, we saw how the absolutely dependent baby steps through autoeroticism towards object relating. When held by the ordinary devoted mother, so as to just "be", a boundary is established where transitional space builds between the nursing and the analytic couples, such that the held baby/patient is able to bridge his inner and outer realities.

In the third chapter, I looked at the second stage of dependence, the prototype transitional space. The nature of transitional phenomena and space was discussed. I saw the mother's successful ego split—being herself whilst being one with her baby—and how she sensitively reduces her adaptation whilst continuing to hold the baby. This way, the baby feels the good effect of his own effort and can risk spontaneity, feel real, contribute to his society, and live an enjoyable and fulfilling life.

In the fourth chapter, the parallel between analysis and infancy still holds in the third stage. Going towards independence, the original transitional space, once internalised, is enriched and expanded in adolescence and adulthood, giving a sense of personal continuity, and taking account of the person's widening interests.

The fifth and sixth chapters provided details of a baby observation and the experience of engaging in a baby observation, and a summarising and reflective report on this baby observation. It is hoped that these bring to life the instances cited in the previous chapters.

Though not within the scope of this volume, it should be acknowledged that the proposed parallel has limits: the immature baby is developing a sense of self for the first time; the cognitively mature adult being held in analysis brings early experiences into the session in order to live them properly. The adult in analysis attempts to experience fully things that could not be borne in the past. Analysis must contend with the legacy of babyhood with all its faults highlighted. All the defence and coping mechanisms—to which the adult has had recourse in order to live—are there too, and will come to life in the space between the patient and the therapist. These aspects of holding are not in the original mother's brief. In the first good enough situation, the baby trusts. In the therapeutic situation, holding may be needed for a very long time before a situation of trust is reached. In the interim, holding will include the therapist's survival of the patient's use of established methods of protecting against impingement.

Winnicott has been criticised for his idiosyncratic and inconsistent use of language, including psychoanalytic terms (Abram, 1996; Phillips, 1988). He uses the terms "true self", "false self", and "secret self" with only loose definition, whilst the concept of self or selves continues today to be a highly controversial one. Although extremely agreeable, his personal style of writing and explanation has been described as resulting in a "peculiar combination of clarity and opacity" (Ogden, 1985). He took no initiative in systematising his psychoanalytic thought and relating it to that of others. He regretted this in later years, acknowledging Masud Khan's help in preparing material for publishing. There is much in Winnicott's style and technique which succeeds by drawing on extraordinary facets of his inimitable personality (Clancier & Kalmanovitch, 1987). A significant amount of what he did was considered psychoanalytically unorthodox and drew scorn, such as the modification of technique and symbol realisation. (Arguments for and against the modification of technique are available in Pedder (1976) and Casement (1982) respectively. Again, they are outside the scope of this book).

There are underdeveloped areas in Winnicott's thinking. Lacan stressed the importance of the paternal function, perhaps at the cost of the mother function. It may be that in attempting to introduce balance in this regard, Winnicott has overshot the mark, leaving the father's role unelaborated. He says that he means the mother's care rather than the actual mother in his writing, and this included the father. He stresses the father's role in being the first separate object with whom the baby can assert his existence in the world. He explains that in primary maternal preoccupation, the father provides necessary holding of the mother, dealing with the greater environment for her. For Winnicott, the father's role with the older child is also important. When the older child begins to assert himself, first within the family and then in the larger society, the father, by his survival, maintains a safe boundary that the older child can internalise, thus avoiding the anti-social tendency. Generally, one may say that the father's function is underplayed, relying perhaps on the classical oedipal situation.

A related and under-explored area is that of sex difference. Winnicott is silent on the effect of the baby's sex on the environment and its consequences. The way in which Winnicott's thinking might take account of the effect of the presence or otherwise of siblings remains unclear, as does the effect of birth order. Other than emphasising the role of experience, expressing his dislike of the concepts of innate envy or the death drive, Winnicott is relatively mute also on the subject of heredity. It is possible to read blame into the great importance that Winnicott, in his writing, attributes to the role of the mother, whereas his intention was to not to apportion blame but to increase our understanding by explanation.

Notwithstanding all of these deficit areas, many valuable theoretical principles and points of technique can be harvested from Winnicott's abundant writing. There is a great deal in Winnicott's rationale that is accessible and replicable, which we can emanate and reproduce to good effect in ordinary clinical practice.

If Anna Freud (1968) was correct in telling Winnicott that he had conquered the analytic world, then that world has grown exponentially since, and his influence within and outside it. The international conference that took place in Massachusetts in June 1987 was "of the high level of multidisciplinary discourse which was in the past reserved for Freud and Lacan" (Grolnick & Barkin, 1998, p. ix).

The territory gained in the fifty years since Winnicott first posited his theory of transitional phenomena includes such exotic sites as "Etruscan burial symbols and the transitional process" and "Poetry as transitional object" (Grolnick & Barkin, 1998). The online database *PsychLit* has thousands of entries for "transitional phenomena" and thirty-nine for "transitional space" in particular. If the usefulness of psychoanalytic concepts and technique is to be measured in the writing of present and future practitioners, then to the evidence in favour of Winnicott's infancy/analysis parallel and transitional concepts already provided, more must be added. Bollas, Casement, Eigen, Green, Khan, Ogden and Phillips are some of the people who are content to acknowledge Winnicott's influence on their psychoanalytic thinking, practice, and writing.

The infancy/analysis parallel is limited. Nevertheless, it should be acknowledged that, along with the concept of transitional phenomena, it has made a very important contribution to psychoanalytic thought. As we have seen with Winnicott's thinking generally, it is clinically useful and has taken many who are currently thinking and practicing psychoanalytically a long way indeed.

REFERENCES

Abraham, K. (1927). A short study of the development of the libido, viewed in the light of mental disorders. In: *Selected Papers of Karl Abraham, M. D.* (pp. 418–501). London: Karnac, 1988.

Abram, J. (1996). *The Language of Winnicott: A Dictionary of Winnicott's Use of Words*. London: Karnac Books.

Balint, M. (1935). Critical notes on the theory of the pregenital organisation of the libido. In: *Primary Love and Psycho-Analytic Technique* (pp. 49–72). London: Karnac, 1994.

Balint, M. (1968). *The Basic Fault: Therapeutic Aspects of Regression*. New York: Brunner/Mazel.

Bion, W. R. (1955). Differentiation of psychotic from nonpychotic personalities. In: E. B. Spillius (Ed.), *Melanie Klein Today Volume 1* (pp. 59–76). London: Routledge, 1988.

Bion, W. R. (1961). A theory of thinking. In: E. B. Spillius (Ed.), *Melanie Klein Today Volume 1* (pp. 174–182). London: Routledge, 1988.

Casement, P. J. (1982). Some pressures on the analyst for physical contact during reliving of an early trauma. In: G. Kohon (Ed.), *The British School of Psychoanalysis: The Independent Tradition* (pp. 282–294). London: Free Association Books, 1986.

Clancier, A. & Kalmanovitch, J. (1987). A splash of paint in his style. In: P. L. Giovacchini (Ed.), *Tactics and Techniques in Psychoanalytic Therapy Volume 3* (pp. 41–59). Northvale, N. J.: Aronson, 1993.

Davenport, G. C. (1994). *An Introduction to Child Development*. London: Collins.

Erikson, E. (1950). *Childhood and Society*. New York: Norton.

Freud, A. (1968). Letter to D. W. Winnicott, 30 October, 1968. In: L. Spurling, *Winnicott Studies No. 11* (p. 44). London: Squiggle Foundation & Karnac.

Freud, S. (1905). *Three essays on the theory of sexuality. S. E.,* 7: 123–246. London: Hogarth.

Freud, S. (1911a). *Psycho-analytical notes on an autobiographical account of a case of paranoia (dementia paranoides). S. E.,* 12: 9–82. London: Hogarth.

Freud, S. (1911b). Formulations on the two principles of mental functioning. *S. E.,* 12: 218–226. London: Hogarth.

Freud, S. (1914). *On narcissism: an introduction. S. E.,* 14: 73–102. London: Hogarth.

Freud, S. (1917). *Mourning and melencholia. S. E.,* 14: 239–258. London: Hogarth.

Freud, S. (1920). *Beyond the Pleasure Principle. S. E.,* 18: 17–64. London: Hogarth.

Freud, S. (1921). *Group Psychology and the Analysis of the Ego. S. E.,* 18: 67–143. London: Hogarth.

Freud, S. (1923). *The Ego and the Id. S. E.,* 19: 3–66. London: Hogarth.

Freud, S. (1924). *The dissolution of the Oedipus complex. S. E.,* 19: 172–179. London: Hogarth.

Freud, S. (1933a). *New Introductory Lectures on Psycho-Analysis. S. E.,* 22: 2–182. London: Hogarth.

Freud, S. (1933b). Femininity. In: *New Introductory Lectures on Psycho-Analysis. S. E.,* 22: 1–182. London: Hogarth.

Giovacchini, P. L. (1990a). Absolute and 'not quite' absolute dependence. In: P. L. Giovacchini (Ed.), *Tactics and Techniques in Psychoanalytic Therapy Volume 3* (pp. 142–159). Northvale, N. J.: Aronson.

Giovacchini, P. L. (1990b). Regression, reconstruction and resolution: containment and holding. In: P. L. Giovacchini. (Ed.), *Tactics and Techniques in Psychoanalytic Therapy Volume 3* (pp. 226–263). Northvale, N. J.: Aronson, 1993.

Goldman, D. (1993). *In Search of the Real: The Origins and Originality of D. W. Winnicott*. Northvale, N. J.: Aronson.

Greenson, R. R. (1995). On transitional objects and transference. In: S. A. Grolnick, L. Barkin & W. Muensterberger (Eds.), *Between Reality and Fantasy: Transitional Objects and Phenomena* (pp. 205–209). Northvale, N. J.: Aronson.

Grolnick, S. A. & Barkin, L. (1988). Preface. In: S. A. Grolnick, L. Barkin & W. Muensterberger (Eds.), *Between Reality and Fantasy: Transitional Objects and Phenomena* (pp. ix–x). Northvale, N. J.: Aronson.

Grosskurth, P. (1986). *Melanie Klein: Her World and her Work*. Northvale, N. J.: Aronson.

Grotstein, J. S. (1990). Introduction. In: M. I. Little (Ed.), *Psychotic Anxiety and Containment: A Personal Record of an Analysis with Winnicott* (pp. 3–11). Northvale, N. J.: Aronson.

Hinshelwood, R. D. (1991). *A Dictionary of Kleinian Thought*. London: Free Association.

Hug-Hellmuth, H. von (1921). On the technique of child-analysis. *International Journal of Psycho-Analysis*, 2: 287–305.

Kahn, M. M. R. (1958). Introduction. In: D. W. Winnicott, *Through Paediatrics to Psychoanalysis* (pp. xi–l). London: Karnac, 1984.

Kahr, B. (1996). *D. W. Winnicott: A Biographical Portrait*. London: Karnac.

Klein, M. (1932). *The Psycho-Analysis of Children*. London: Virago, 1989.

Klein, M. (1935). A Contribution to the psychogenesis of manic-depressive states. In: J. Mitchell (Ed.), *The Selected Melanie Klein* (pp. 262–289). London: Penguin, 1991.

Klein, M. (1940). Mourning and its relation to manic-depressive states. In: J. Mitchell (Ed.), *The Selected Melanie Klein* (pp. 344–369). London: Penguin. 1991.

Klein, M. (1946). Notes on some schizoid mechanisms. In: *Envy and Gratitude* (pp. 1–24). London: Vintage, 1988.

Klein, M. (1952). The origins of transference. In: *Envy and Gratitude* (pp. 48–56). London: Virago, 1988.

Klein, M. (1957). Envy and gratitude. In: *Envy and Gratitude* (pp. 176–235). London: Virago, 1988.

Laplanche, J. & Pontalis, J. -B., (1973). *The Language of Psychoanalysis*. London: Karnac.

Little, M. I. (1990). *Psychotic Anxiety and Containment: A Personal Record of an Analysis with Winnicott*. Northvale, N. J.: Aronson.

Mendez, A. & Fine, R. (1976). A short history of the British school of object relations and ego psychology. *Bulletin of Menninger Clinic, 40*: 357–382.

Mitchell, J. (1991). Introduction. In: J. Mitchell (Ed.), *The Selected Melanie Klein*. London: Virago.

Ogden, T. (1985). On potential space. In: P. L. Giovacchini. (Ed.), *Tactics and Techniques in Psychoanalytic Therapy Volume 3* (pp. 90–112). Northvale, N. J.: Aronson, 1993.

Parrish, D. (1995). Transitional objects and phenomena in a case of twinship. In: S. A. Grolnick, L. Barkin & W. Muensterberger (Eds.), *Between Reality and Fantasy: Transitional Objects and Phenomena* (pp. 273–287). Northvale, N. J.: Aronson.

Phillips, A. (1988). *Winnicott*. London: Fontana.

Pedder, J. R. (1976). Attachment and new beginning. In: G. Kohon (Ed.), *The British School of Psychoanalysis: The Independent Tradition* (pp. 295–308). London: Free Association, 1986.

Rodman, F. R. (1987). Introduction. In: F. R. Rodman (Ed.), *The Spontaneous Gesture: Selected Letters of D. W. Winnicott* (pp. xiii–xxxiii). London: Karnac.

Rodman, F. R. (1999). *The Spontaneous Gesture: Selected Letters of D. W. Winnicott*. London: Karnac.

Rodman, F. R. (2003). *Winnicott: His Life and Work*. Cambridge, MA: Perseus.

Sartre, J. -P. (1957). *Being and Nothingness* (Trans. H. Barnes). London: Methuen.

Sweden, R. C. van (1995). *Regression to Dependence: A Second Opportunity for Ego Integration and Developmental Progression*. New York: Aronson.

Volkan, V. D. & Kavanaugh, J. G. (1995). The cat people. In: S. A. Grolnick, L. Barkin & W. Muensterberger (Eds.), *Between Reality and Fantasy: Transitional Objects and Phenomena* (pp. 289–303). Northvale, N. J.: Aronson.

Winnicott, D. W. (1935). The manic defence. In: *Through Paediatrics to Psychoanalysis* (pp. 129–144). London: Karnac, 1984.

Winnicott, D. W. (1941). The observation of infants in a set situation. In: *Through Paediatrics to Psychoanalysis* (pp. 52–69). London: Karnac, 1984.

Winnicott, D. W. (1942). Why children play. In: *The Child, the Family and the Outside World* (pp. 143–146). London: Penguin, 1991.

Winnicott, D. W. (1945). Primative emotional development. In: *Through Paediatrics to Psychoanalysis* (pp. 145–154). London: Karnac, 1984 .

Winnicott, D. W. (1947). Hate in the countertransference. In: *Through Paediatrics to Psychoanalysis* (pp. 194–203). London: Karnac, 1984.

Winnicott, D. W. (1949). The world in small doses. In: *The Child, The Family and the Outside World* (pp. 69–74). London: Penguin, 1991.

Winnicott, D. W. (1951). Transitional objects and transitional phenomena. In: *Through Paediatrics to Psychoanalysis* (pp. 229–242). London: Karnac, 1984.

Winnicott, D. W. (1952). Anxiety associated with insecurity. In: *Through Paediatrics to Psychoanalysis* (pp. 97–100). London: Karnac, 1984.

Winnicott, D. W. (1953). Transitional objects and transitional phenomena. In: *Playing and Reality* (pp. 1–34). London: Routledge, 1971.

Winnicott, D. W. (1954). Metapsychological and clinical aspects of regression within the psycho-analytical set-up. In: *Through Paediatrics to Psychoanalysis* (pp. 278–295). London: Karnac, 1984.

Winnicott, D. W. (1955). Group influences and the maladjusted child. In: C. Winnicott, R. Shepherd & M. Davis (Eds.), *Deprivation and Delinquency* (pp. 189–199). London: Tavistock, 1984.

Winnicott, D. W. (1956). Primary maternal preoccupation. In: *Through Paediatrics to Psychoanalysis* (pp. 300–305). London: Karnac, 1984.

Winnicott, D. W. (1960a). The theory of the parent–infant relationship. In: *Maturational Processes and the Facilitating Environment* (pp. 37–55). London: Karnac, 1984.

Winnicott, D. W. (1960b). String: A technique of communication. In: *Maturational Processes and the Facilitating Environment* (pp. 153–157). London: Karnac, 1984.

Winnicott, D. W. (1962a). A personal view of the Kleinian contribution. In: *Maturational Processes and the Facilitating Environment* (pp. 171–178). London: Karnac, 1984.

Winnicott, D. W. (1962b). Providing for the child in health and crises. In: *Maturational Processes and the Facilitating Environment* (pp. 64–72). London: Karnac, 1984.

Winnicott, D. W. (1962c). Ego integration in child development. In: *Maturational Processes and the Facilitating Environment* (pp. 56–63). London: Karnac, 1984.

Winnicott, D. W. (1963a). Fear of breakdown. In: C. Winnicott, R. Shepherd & M. Davis (Eds.), *Psycho-Analytic Explorations* (pp. 87–95). London: Karnac, 1989.

Winnicott, D. W. (1963b). From dependence towards independence in the development of the individual. In: *Maturational Processes and the Facilitating Environment* (pp. 83–92). London: Karnac, 1984.

Winnicott, D. W. (1963c). On "The use of an object". In: C. Winnicott, R. Shepherd & M. Davis (Eds.), *Psycho-Analytic Explorations* (pp. 217–246). London: Karnac, 1989.

Winnicott, D. W. (1963d). The development of the capacity for concern. In: *Maturational Processes and the Facilitating Environment* (pp. 73–82). London: Karnac, 1984.

Winnicott, D. W. (1967a). Mirror-role of mother and family in child development. In *Playing and Reality* (pp. 149–159). London: Routledge, 1971.

Winnicott, D. W. (1967b). The location of cultural experience. In: *Playing and Reality* (pp. 128–139). London: Routledge, 1971.

Winnicott, D. W. (1968). Communication between infant and mother and mother and infant, compared and contrasted. In: C. Winnicott,

R. Shepherd & M. Davis (Eds.), *Babies and Their Mothers* (pp. 89–103). London: Free Association, 1988.

Winnicott, D. W. (1969). The use of an object in the context of Moses and monotheism. In: C. Winnicott, R. Shepherd & M. Davis (Eds.), *Psycho-Analytic Explorations* (pp. 240–246). London: Karnac, 1989.

Winnicott, D. W. (1971a). Playing: creative activity and the search for self. In: *Playing and Reality* (pp. 71–86). London: Routledge, 1971.

Winnicott, D. W. (1971b). Dreaming, fantasying and living: a case-history describing a primary dissociation. In: *Playing and Reality* (pp. 35–50). London: Routledge, 1971.

Winnicott, D. W. (1971c). Playing: a theoretical statement. In: *Playing and Reality* (pp. 51–70). London: Routledge, 1971.

Winnicott, D. W. (1989). *Holding and Interpretation: Fragment of an Analysis*. London: Karnac.

Winnicott, D. W. (1996). *Therapeutic Consultations in Child Psychiatry* London: Karnac.

Wright, K. (1991). *Vision and Separation: Between Mother and Baby*. Northvale, N. J.: Aronson.

INDEX